MARY'S YES FROM AGE TO AGE

Mary's Yes

from
Age to Age

John E. Rotelle, O.S.A.

with an introduction
by

Cardinal Michele Pellegrino

Collins

Collins Liturgical Publications
8 Grafton Street, London W1X 3LA

© in the compilation John Rotelle 1988
ISBN 0 00 599170 6
First Published 1989

Typesetting by Exordium, Washington, DC
Made and printed by William Collins Sons & Co Ltd,
      Glasgow

Acknowledgements

pages 103-104, Meister Eckhart, The Essential Sermons, Commentaries, Treatises, and Defense, The Classic of Western Spirituality, Paulist Press, 1986, pages 192-193.

page 114, Johannes Tauler, Sermons, The Classics of Western Spirituality, Paulist Press, 1985, page 39.

page 118, Catherine of Siena, The Dialogue, The Classics of Western Spirituality, Paulist Press, 1980, page 286.

page 119, John Ruusbroec, The Spiritual Espousals and Other Works, The Classics of Western Spirituality, 1985, pages 225-226.

pages 120-121, Julian of Norwich, Showings, The Classics of Western Spirituality, Paulist Press, 1978, pages 131, 187, 292.

page 175, A. Hulsbosch, O.S.A., God's Creation, Sheed and Ward, 1965.

page 178, Karl Rahner, Mary, Mother of the Lord, Herder and Herder, New York, 1963.

page 181, Pierre Grelot, La Bible, Parole de Dieu, Desclee, Tournai, 1965.

page 182, Réné Voillaume, Demeures de Dieu, l'Eglise, la Vierge, Le Cerf, Paris, 1954.

page 183, Réné Laurentin, Court Traite sur la Vierge Marie, Lethielleux, Paris, 1967

page 184, Raymond E. Brown, The Community of the Beloved Disciple, Paulist Press, New York, 1979.

page 185, Joseph Ratzinger, Dogma and Preaching, Franciscan Herald Press, 1985.

page 186, Edward Schillebeeckx, Mary, Mother of the Redemption, Sheed and Ward, New York, 1964.

Dedicated to the memory
of my
beloved grandparents

John Rotelle

and

Antonia Riccardelli Rotelle

whose little statue of Mary
was my first introduction
to
Mary, the Mother of God

Contents

Foreword

Throughout the centuries Mary's yes to the angel of God has found an echo in the hearts of many women and men. It is no wonder that many have taken pen in hand to extol, explain, and be thankful for her response to the angel.

Several years ago when I thought of this book, I began to collect texts of Church documents and Christian writers. When Pope John Paul II announced the Marian Year, it seemed opportune to begin to gather the results of my work. Originally I had planned to present the texts with an introduction. Yet when I examined each text in its historical setting, I began to see a chain of interlocking ideas in Marian thought, like mountains and valleys, linking one century to another. What startled me the most was the influence of Augustine and the Augustinian school on Marian theology and devotion. I knew that Augustine, unlike later Church writers, said little on Mary as such, but I was constantly seeing his influence in councils, on writers, and in theology. For this reason I chose to use the two beautiful conferences of Cardinal Pellegrino which he gave some years ago at the Angelicum in Rome. In that introduction the Cardinal outlined the salient features of Augustine's thought on Mary. From the collected texts one can readily see that Augustine laid the foundation for much of Marian thought in subsequent centuries.

Through the first nine centuries the figure of Mary was developed in relation to the great events of salvation history. Writers like Irenaeus, Augustine, and Bernard emphasized Mary's obedience to God's will and thus becoming the new Eve reversing the disobedience of Eve, and the Virgin Mary's role as mother of the Savior and as Mother of God. Emphasis on Mary in this era was doctrinal and liturgical. Mary was acclaimed as God-bearer, Theotokos, and was seen as a type of the Church.

At the time of the growth of monasteries in the eleventh and twelfth centuries, private prayers and individual devotions developed widely. Pilgrims and travelers spread these practices from one place to another, and the previous emphasis on Mary as Theotokos or type of the Church shifted to focus on the person, Mary, in relation to herself.

As the cultural emphases shifted from the rural to the urban, from country to cities, the spread of faith was associated with the rise of the mendicant orders whose work was focused in the cities and in the universities. The monastic setting for the faith gave way to Christian life in the city and town. Itinerant preachers thus brought the richness of their contemplation to towns and cities, preaching the gospel to serve their needs.

Spirituality took on a different shape. The human dimensions of Jesus began to be highlighted more fully. Because of wars, pestilence, and schism the penitential aspects of Christianity were brought into focus, and Mary was seen as Mother of Mercy, the one who cares for and intercedes for her children. Devotional practices continued to increase. From monastic cloisters they had been diffused through Christian cities with the itinerant friars. Now they were taken up by the clergy and then by the people. Mary became their mediator in time of need, their mother to whom they called out.

There was no uniformity; much variety existed from country to country. At certain peak moments there was agreement, usually given formal expression in dogmas or council documents. Usually these decisions signaled the end of an emphasis on one aspect of Mary's role or personality and the planting of a new idea or emphasis.

The university professors of this era, although their writing was strongly scholastic and somewhat dry, nonetheless managed to speak about Mary, the mother of Jesus, in intimate, even devotional terms.

In the era of reform, the fifteenth to the seventeenth centuries, the abuses that had accumulated were rightly bemoaned, especially the invocation of Mary when in distress to the point of ignoring God. Saints and great writers honored the Blessed Virgin while at the same time pleading for correction of abuses and exaggerations.

The reformers who had been nurtured on devotion to Mary in their Catholic lives did not abandon this devotion, but, like others, called for an end to exaggerations and abuses. Martin Luther, an Augustinian friar, took the lead in this. For this reason some of his inspiring writings have been included in this book. Later reformers took a more severe direction concerning Marian devotion.

From the eighteenth century onward there was a marked increase in devotion to Mary. Excesses and abuses were still present, but a cry for reform also persisted. Many lamented the fact that the centrality of Christ's incarnation had been put aside. Yet even in some of the most ardent Marian devotees of this period, a recognition of Christ's role was present. That can be seen in Bartolomé de los Rios, Louis de Montfort, and Alfonsus Liguori.

Today, especially since the Second Vatican Council, there is a call for an end to exaggeration and abuse in Marian devotion. It is a call to emphasize the centrality of the mystery of Christ's coming in the flesh. There is also a growing trend, especially in the liturgical context, to honor and highlight Mary's sublime role as Mother of God.

The pivotal points of difficulty or tension within the Christian churches are the role of Mary as mediatrix and as queen. While some would agree that these aspects are legitimate extensions of Mary's role at the beginning of Christ's life, others would maintain that these obscure the christological thrust of Mary's role.

From the texts presented in this book two things can be noted. First, different writers in diverse times with a variety of images and expressions present Mary's reply and her role in salvation history as the focus of their work. Her role as Mother of God always stands out, even in the periods when Marian devotion was most prominent. Secondly, the influence of Saint Augustine's thought was naturally great, and this comes as no surprise. In the year after his death, 431, his authority was given prominence by Pope Celestine I:

> We have always held Augustine a man of holy memory because of his life and also because of his services in our communion, nor has even report ever sullied him with unfavorable suspicion. We recall him as having once been a man of such great knowledge that even by my predecessors in the past he was always accounted among the best teachers.

Ever since that time the influence of Augustine has graced the Church. His own writing, *The Gift of Perseverance,* tries to put his contribution in perspective:

> I would not wish anyone so to esteem my writings that he would follow me except in those matters in which he has clearly seen I do not err. For on this account I am now composing books in which I have undertaken to examine my works, so that I may show that I myself have not conformed to myself in all things (21, 55).

What did astound me is the role that the Augustinian School (followers of Augustine and admirers of his thought) has played in Marian devotion throughout the centuries. At each peak moment of Marian devotion Augustine's authority or someone from the Augustinian school was involved. In passages here selected and in those which I could not include here, time and time again Augustine was recalled. This is not to minimize the important roles of Bernard, Anselm, Amadeus, or others; rather it shows the progression of thought which is built on the shoulders of each giant of the century. Some giants, however, step into each century.

It is my hope that this book will help believers to follow the example of Mary and to say their own yes to God's plan in their lives. Likewise may all Christians cherish Mary as their mother.

John E. Rotelle, O.S.A.
20 February 1988

How to Use this Book

While this book may be read from cover to cover, it is suggested that it be used for prayer or reflection. For this reason, after the introduction, each page is a self-contained unit even though a reading may be continued. You may wish to read a page at a time, for example, a page a day or a page when you pick up the book. It is best to read it consecutively, that is, from the second century to the twentieth century. In this way one sees very vividly the impact of Mary's yes from age to age.

Introduction

Cardinal Michele Pellegrino

Mary in the Thought of Saint Augustine

Augustine's Presentation of Marian Themes

IN EXEGESIS

As we read through writings of Augustine that deal with Marian themes, it soon becomes evident that exegesis most often serves as the point of departure and leads to the fullest treatments. By "exegesis" here I do not mean simply the writer's scholarly explanations of passages in scripture; I include also those expositions of the revealed word that are suggested by his catechetical, polemical, or pastoral concerns. I turn now to the passages of scripture which most frequently serve the Saint as a springboard for discussion of Mary (I follow the traditional order of the books of the Bible):

Old Testament

In the *earth of paradise* (or the "face of the earth") which no human being tilled and which was watered by a spring (Genesis 2:5f.) Augustine sees a figure of the Virgin Mary, who was watered by the Holy Spirit and from whom Jesus was born without human cooperation (*Answer to Faustus* II, 37).

The *formation of the first woman* from the side of the first man without carnal union is paralleled with the virginal birth of Christ from his handmaid (*The Literal Meaning of Genesis* IX, 30; *Sermon* 51, 3).

Some passages of the psalms are connected with Mary. Her womb is the bridal chamber from which Jesus comes forth like a bridegroom to run his way rejoicing (Psalm 18[19]:6), that is, to celebrate his marriage to the Church (*Homilies on the Gospel of John* 8, 4; Sermon 51, 2; 291, 6). Mary is the earth that gives birth to the Truth (Psalm 84[85]:12), that is, Christ himself (Sermon 191, 2; Sermon 189, 2).

Augustine more than once refers to the passage in Isaiah: *Who shall describe his generation?* (Isaiah 53:8; see Acts 8:33) not only to the eternal generation of the Word from the Father but also to the temporal birth of Jesus from Mary; this birth is rendered even more ineffable by the marvelous virginity of the mother (Sermon 195, 1; 196, 1; 215, 3).

In the Book of Daniel an allusion to Mary is suggested by the stone that is cut from the mountain without human hand (Daniel 2:34), for this stone prefigures Jesus, who was born of the Virgin without marital intercourse (*Homilies on the Gospel of John* 9, 15). There is also a parallel between Susanna and Mary: as Daniel, inspired by the Holy Spirit, intervened to save Susanna from a groundless suspicion of infidelity, so an angel intervened to save Mary from unjustified suspicion by her husband (Sermon 343, 3-4).

New Testament

Among the New Testament passages that provide Augustine with an occasion for speaking of the Virgin we may distinguish those that are part of the gospel narrative and those that are properly doctrinal, although we must bear in mind that the doctrinal element emerges quite naturally as an interpretation of the historical narrative.

Narrative passages

Augustine discusses the genealogy of Jesus not only in order to resolve the difficulties caused by the discrepancies between Matthew and Luke, but also to show that Jesus truly is what the scriptures say he is: a son of David. He does so by pointing out that while the two evangelists trace Jesus back to David through Joseph, Mary, the true mother of the Redeemer, was also somehow connected with the tribe of Judah and had the blood of David in her veins (*Agreement among the Evangelists* 2, 4; Sermon 51, 20, 30).

Augustine's commentary on the announcement of the angel to Mary aims at proving that Mary had consecrated her virginity to the Lord by a vow, as well as at bringing out her greatness and humility and the faith with which she believed in God's word (Sermon 51, 18; 215, 2; 291, 5-6).

I mentioned earlier the *suspicions* roused in Joseph by his wife's pregnancy, and how these were removed by the angel (Sermon 343).

A reference to the purification of Mary occurs in a passage in which Augustine excludes the need of such a cleansing in her case (*Questions on the Heptateuch* 3, 40).

In the words which Mary addresses to Jesus in the temple: *Your father and I have been looking for you anxiously,* Augustine finds evidence of the modesty of Mary, since she gives first place to her husband (Sermon 51, 11-18).

The answer of Jesus to Mary at the wedding in Cana: *Woman, what have you to do with me? My hour has not yet come* creates two problems for Augustine the exegete. The first is that the word *mulier* was interpreted by some (probably the Manicheans) as a denial of the true motherhood of Mary, since Jesus (they said) refuses to call her "Mother." But (Augustine points out) the words at the beginning of the narrative: *and the mother of Jesus was there,* are a complete refutation of this heretical interpretation (*Homilies on the Gospel of John* 8, 4-9).

The second problem is that the tone of Jesus' reply seems at first glance lacking in reverence for Mary. This, however, is explained when we realize that on this occasion Jesus wishes to focus attention on his divinity, which enables him to perform the miracle. But "as God he did not have a mother," while "as man he had one"; Mary was "the mother of his flesh, mother of his humanity, mother of the weakness which he assumed for our sake" (*ibid.*).

The gospel offers a further difficulty when it speaks of the *brothers* of Jesus (Matthew 12:46-50; John 2:21). In explaining the second of these two passages Augustine appeals to a peculiarity of biblical language, which gives the name *brothers* even to cousins; he simply denies that Mary had other children after Jesus (*Homilies on the Gospel of John* 10, 2-3; see 28, 3).

The passage in Matthew, which tells of the mother and brothers of Jesus wanting to speak with him and gives Jesus' answer: *Who is my mother, and who are my brothers?* is the subject of a lengthy commentary in a sermon. After acknowledging the difficulty which the passage causes, Augustine shows that the words of Jesus are not an insult to his mother. In speaking as he does of her who sought him out while he was absorbed in the work of God, the Savior wished to teach the proper order required by charity, for love of God takes priority over every human affection (*Sermon 72A, 3-4*).

When commenting on the passage in which John the evangelist tells how the dying Jesus entrusted Mary to him (John 19:24-27), Augustine repeats an observation he has already made in connection with the wedding in Cana: on the cross, when about to die, Jesus acknowledges the mother of his weakness (*Homilies on the Gospel of John* 109, 1).

Doctrinal passages

Mary is mentioned when Augustine comments on certain New Testament texts that are especially important for the mystery of the incarnation. As we shall see, he likes to emphasize the essential role which the Virgin played in the divine plan.

The prologue of the gospel of John, and especially the words: *The Word was made flesh and dwelt among us* (John 1:14), give Augustine an opportunity to point out the mysterious connection between the eternal generation of the Word from the Father and the temporal birth of Jesus from Mary (Sermon 195, 3; *Homilies on the Gospel of John* 110, 3; Sermon 214, 6; 215, 3; 291, 6; Sermon 110, 3). They also enable him to emphasize the reality of the human nature which the Word willed to assume from Mary for our sake (Sermon 279, 7).

There is a passage in the Letter to the Romans in which Paul says: *God sent his own Son in the likeness of sinful flesh* (Romans 8:3). Augustine explains that the body of Christ was not sinful flesh but only a likeness of it because it was conceived by Mary without the intervention of concupiscence (*The Literal Meaning of Genesis* 10, 38; Sermon 69, 4; *Answer to Julian* 5, 15, 51).

Another passage in Paul: *made of a woman, made under the law* (Galatians 4:4), shows that Jesus is truly the son of Mary (*Homilies on the Gospel of John* 8, 9). On the other hand, the word *mulier,* used here for *woman,* should not make us think of a loss of virginity, since in Hebrew usage *mulier* was synonymous with *femina* (*Homilies on the Gospel of John* 10, 2; Sermon 51, 11, 18).

IN CONTROVERSY

Biblical exegesis (in the sense given the term earlier) provides Augustine with his most frequent opportunities for discussing mariological themes. Such themes are, on the contrary, usually only suggested by the requirements of controversy or catechetical instruction.

At times Augustine's arguments are aimed at the *pagans*. On one occasion, Marcellinus, a tribune, had laid before him the objections raised by Volusian to the virginity of Mary. In reply, after proving her virginity, Augustine appeals, in an *ad hominem* argument, to similar wonders narrated in pagan literature (Letter 143, 12). On another occasion, he asserts against the "Platonists" the marvelous appropriateness of Christ's virginal birth from Mary (*The City of God* 10, 29).

Against the *Manicheans*, who denied the reality of Christ's earthly body and therefore of his birth from Mary, Augustine reaffirms both with an appeal to the gospel (*Answer to Faustus* 26, 7; see *Answer to Two Letters of the Pelagians* 1, 2, 4; *Answer to Julian* 1, 2, 4).

Augustine's earlier-mentioned attempt to show that Mary was in some degree a member of the tribe of David was likewise aimed at the Manicheans. It was directed, in particular, at Faustus, their "bishop," who had adopted the objections of the pagan controversialists and used to claim that if Jesus were indeed descended from David he must have been the natural son of Joseph, since only the latter's line is traced back to David in the genealogies of the gospels (*Answer to Faustus* 23, 8-9).

Against *Jovinian* and the *Helvidians* (whom he identifies with the *Antidicomarians*) Augustine vigorously defends the perpetual virginity of Mary (*Heresies* 56, 82 and 84; see *Answer to Two Letters of the Pelagians* 1, 2, 4; *Answer to Julian* 1, 2, 4; *Unfinished Work in Answer to Julian* 4, 122).

IN INSTRUCTION

Marian themes emerge in three contexts that are closely connected with catechesis or basic instruction in the faith:

First and foremost there are the references to the "rule of faith" (*regula fidei*: Sermon 186, 2), which Augustine also calls the "order and text of our faith" (Sermon 51, 18). He cites the relevant section with some variations: "We profess him to have been born of the Holy Spirit and the Virgin Mary" (Sermon 51, 18; Sermon 214, 6; Sermon 229P); "who was conceived of the Holy Spirit, born of the Virgin Mary" (Sermon 213, 2); "born of the Holy Spirit from the Virgin Mary" (Sermon 215, 4); "we believe in the Son of God who was born of the Virgin Mary" (Sermon 186, 2).

The "rule of faith" serves Augustine as an argument for the perpetual virginity of Mary; for a distinction between the action of the Holy Spirit, who sanctifies, and the action of Mary, who conceives and gives birth; and as proof of the divine maternity of Mary, since he who was born of her is truly the Son of God.

Some of the references just cited to the rule of faith occur in sermons dealing with *moments of special importance in catechesis.* I refer to sermons given on occasion of the "handing over of the creed" (*traditio symboli*): for example, Sermon 213, which explains the parallel between Mary and the Church, or Sermon 214; and to sermons subsequently given when the creed was recited or "given back" (*redditio symboli*): for example, Sermon 215.

I shall mention, finally, sermons given on some more solemn feasts: not only those on the feast of the Nativity of Jesus (Sermons 184, 186-189, 190-96), but also those on the birth of John the Baptist (Sermons 290, 291) and some of those dealing with Easter (Sermons 223D, 225, 232).

Prominent Themes
in the Mariology of Saint Augustine

Saint Augustine's writings admittedly do not give evidence of a systematic teaching about Mary. They do, however, provide an abundant material in this area, and we may legitimately try to organize it by following an outline now familiar in theology.

MARY IN THE DIVINE PLAN

In commenting on the answer which Jesus gives to Mary at Cana: *My hour has not yet come,* Augustine remarks that while the Redeemer does not give recognition to his mother on this occasion, he will do so later on Calvary. He adds: "Before he was born of her, he had acknowledged his mother by predestining her; and before he himself as God had created her, he knew the mother from whom he would be born as a man" (*Homilies on the Gospel of John* 8, 9).

Augustine also points out that Christ chose his own mother (Sermon 69, 4; 72A, 7; 110; 186, 1; 188, 3; 190, 1; 192, 1; 215, 3; *Holy Virginity* 4; *The Merits and Forgiveness of Sins* 2, 38); that the Word prepared for himself the woman who was to be his virginal mother on earth (*Answer to Faustus* 23, 10); and that he bestowed abundant graces on her (*Nature and Grace* 36).

MARY IN HER EARTHLY LIFE

As I noted earlier, exegesis and controversy required Augustine to concern himself on more than one occasion with the earthly origin of Mary. He claims that she belonged to a priestly family because she was a cousin of Elizabeth, who, according to Luke (1:5), was one of *the daughters of Aaron;* and that she had some ties of blood with David, because Paul says (Romans 1:3) that according to the flesh Christ was descended from David (*Agreement among the Evangelists* 2, 4; see *Homilies on the Gospel of John* 8, 9; *Miscellany of 83 Questions* 61, 2).

In this matter, Augustine rejects the testimony of the apocryphal New Testament, and specifically the *Protoevangelium of James,* to which Faustus the Manichean appealed. This document makes Mary the daughter of a priest named Joachim; even then, however, the father of Mary must have somehow been connected with the posterity of David (*Answer to Faustus* 23, 9).

Of Mary's bodily appearance Augustine admits that we know nothing (*The Trinity* 8, 7). Mary was truly the *wife of Joseph,* whose marital authority she willingly recognized. She was united to him not by fleshly bonds but by affection of mind and heart (Sermon 51, 18; *Answer to Faustus* 23, 8; *Marriage and Desire* 11, 12).

In a passing reference to Mary's visit to Elizabeth Augustine numbers Mary among the final prophets, coming before John the Baptist (*The City of God* 17, 24).

Showing by his own example the care children should take of their parents, the dying Jesus gave Mary another son, as it were, to replace himself. This new son was John, who took her *into his home.* This phrase does not mean that John owned anything of his own; the sense is rather that the disciple and servant took care of the mother of his Teacher and Lord and provided for her needs out of what he himself received when the common stores of the faithful were distributed (*Homilies on the Gospel of John* 109, 3).

MARY IN THE HISTORY OF SALVATION

It is natural that theologians should be interested chiefly in this aspect of Mary, for it is here that the divine plan regarding her emerges clearly.

Mother of the Redeemer

As was noted earlier, Augustine asserts and defends the genuine motherhood of Mary chiefly in debate with the Manicheans, who were docetists. The reality of Mary's motherhood is inseparable from the reality of the incarnation and redemption. If the gospel were lying when it calls Mary the mother of Jesus (John 2:1), it would also be lying when it reports his suffering and death: "If the mother is not real, then neither is the flesh or the wounds of the passion or the scars of the risen Lord, and it is not truth but falsehood that will set free those who believe in him" (*Homilies on the Gospel of John* 8, 7).

In the homily just cited, the real motherhood of Mary is proved, as the passage shows, by an appeal to the gospel: *The mother of Jesus was there* (this point is made even more strongly in the *Answer to Faustus* 26, 7). Elsewhere Augustine invokes the earlier mentioned passage in the Letter to the Galatians (4:4): *made of a woman.*

The sense in which the "motherhood" of Mary is to be understood is explained repeatedly: "Our Lord Jesus Christ was God and man: as God he did not have a mother; as man he had one. Mary was therefore mother of the flesh, mother of the humanity, mother of the weakness which he assumed for our sake" (*Homilies on the Gospel of John* 8, 9; see 119, 1).

This careful distinction does not prevent Augustine from professing, in language that is clearly equivalent, the traditional faith in the divine motherhood of Mary, which was to be solemnly defined at Ephesus a year after his death. Not only does he rebuke those who try to prove that the Son of God was not born of a woman (*The Christian Combat* 24). Not only does he say that Mary gave birth to her Lord (Sermon 51, 20), the Lord of heaven and earth (Sermon 193, 1) and that Mary's Creator was born of her (Sermon 187, 4). He does not even hesitate to say: "God was born of a woman" (*The Trinity* 5, 7).

Elsewhere he specifies the precise theological reason for the dogma of Mary's divine motherhood, namely, the union in Christ of God and man. He says that in Mary's womb the divine nature was united to the human (Sermon 195, 3), and he explains:

> When the Word became flesh, he was not destroyed by coming in the flesh; rather the flesh drew near to the Word, while itself not being destroyed. The result: just as a human being is soul and flesh, so Christ is God and man. The same person who is God is also a man: not by a confusion of the two natures but by their union in the one person. In short, one and the same person who as Son of God is always from the Father and coeternal with his begetter began to be a son of man through birth from the virgin. . . .
>
> Indeed, how could we say in the rule of faith that we believe in the Son of God who was born of the Virgin Mary, unless the Son of God and not simply the son of man were born of the virgin Mary? After all, what Christian denies that the son of man was born of this woman?! (Sermon 186, 2).
>
> Elizabeth conceived a man, Mary conceived a man. Elizabeth was mother of John, Mary was mother of Christ. But whereas Elizabeth conceived only a man, Mary conceived both God and a man. What an astounding thing: that a creature could have conceived its Creator! (Sermon 189, 2; see also Sermon 51, 26; 188, 2).

The importance of Mary's motherhood in the economy of the Christian mystery is seen as residing in the essential connection between this prerogative and the incarnation. The womb of the Virgin is the marriage chamber from which the bridegroom emerges rejoicing at the wedding of the Word and flesh (Sermon 195, 3; *Homilies on the Gospel of John* 8, 4; Sermon 291, 6).

Elsewhere the significance of this privilege is underscored by the close participation of Mary in the work of the Holy Spirit; by the marvels which the mystery of the incarnation implies (Sermon 225, 2-3); by the greatness of the Word of God, who is "the Day that shines on the angels, the Day that illumines the fatherland from which we are exiled," but who nonetheless "clothed himself in flesh and was born of Mary the virgin" (Sermon 189, 2); by the parallel between the birth of Christ from the Virgin and the generation of the Word from the Father: "The generation of Christ from the Father takes place without a mother; the generation of Christ from his mother took place without a father" (Sermon 189, 4; see also Sermon 192, 1; 194, 1; 195, 3). Therefore the birth from Mary, who is both virgin and mother, is "celebrated not by little old ladies with human festivities but by the gospels with divine praises" (Sermon 193, 1).

Mother and Virgin

An unparalleled trait of the motherhood of Mary is its conjunction with the privilege of complete and perpetual virginity. Augustine everywhere asserts and defends this prerogative, whether to refute the heretics who deny it, or to remind his audience of the great miracle involved, or to discourse on the lofty example it gives.

I shall indicate first some passages in which the virginity of Mary is proclaimed in a comprehensive way, that is, without focusing on particular aspects or phases of it. "As a virgin she conceived, as a virgin she gave birth, a virgin she remained" (Sermon 51, 18). "A virgin in conception, a virgin in birth, a virgin in pregnancy, a virgin for ever" (Sermon 186, 1). "Let us therefore celebrate with rejoicing the day on which Mary gave birth to the Savior: a wife to the author of marriage, a virgin to the prince of virgins, a married woman with a husband yet a mother without a husband; a virgin before marriage, a virgin in marriage, a virgin in pregnancy, a virgin who suckled a child" (Sermon 188, 4). "Who can comprehend the utterly anomalous and unparalleled novelty, the unbelievable event that has become believable and is, astoundingly, believed throughout the world: a virgin conceiving, a virgin giving birth and, though giving birth, remaining a virgin?" (Sermon 190, 2). "A virgin conceived: be amazed! A virgin gave birth: be even more amazed! And after giving birth she remained a virgin" (Sermon 196, 1).

In other passages Augustine asserts the virginity of Mary in its several stages: *before giving birth* (Sermon 343, 3; *The Christian Combat* 22, 24); *in giving birth* (*Handbook* 34, 10; *The Trinity* 8, 7; *Heresies* 82; *Unfinished Work in Answer to Julian* 4, 122, especially against Helvidius and Jovinian; and *after giving birth*: "Just as the tomb in which the Lord's body was laid held no other dead person before or after him, so the womb of Mary conceived no other human being before or after him" (*Homilies on the Gospel of John* 28, 3; almost identical language in Sermon 223D, 2; *Heresies* 56; 84; *Marriage and Desire* 2, 5, 15).

It is easy to list many passages in which Augustine mentions the virginity of Mary in passing or formally affirms and defends it; see *On Genesis: A Refutation of the Manicheans* 2, 37; *The Literal Meaning of Genesis* 9, 30; *Agreement among the Evangelists* 2, 2; *Homilies on the Gospel of John* 9, 15; Sermon

69, 3; Sermon 72A, 3; Sermon 110, 3; 187, 4; Sermon 189, 2; 191, 1-4; 192, 1-2; 195, 1-2; 213, 7; 214, 6; 215, 3-4; 290, 6; 291, 5-6; *The Instruction of Beginners* 40; *The Excellence of Marriage* 35).

Saint Augustine repeatedly claims that Mary remained a virgin in fulfillment of an explicit promise, a *vow* by which she consecrated herself irrevocably to the Lord: "Because she had promised virginity ... she said in response to the angel's announcement: *How can this be, since I do not know any man?* (Luke 1:34). If it had been her intention to have knowledge of a man, she would not have been surprised. ... Her surprise is proof of her promise" (Sermon 215, 2; see also Sermon 291, 5). It was this vow, pronounced at a time when the ideal of virginity was still unknown, that made her acceptable in God's sight (*Holy Virginity* 4).

Role in the Economy of Salvation

The fact that Mary became the mother of Christ gave her a unique role in the economy of redemption, because it was through her mediation that the Savior entered the world. Augustine finds this idea foreshadowed in the hymn of the angels at Bethlehem: "A cry of festive rejoicing, not only for the woman whose womb had brought a son into the world but for the human race, for whose sake the Virgin had given birth to the Savior" (Sermon 193, 1).

In a flight of poetic fancy Augustine uses the image of a star to express the mission of Mary as harbinger of redemption. He says that "among that people [he is referring to the Hebrews] the Virgin Mary was not a 'night' but rather 'a star of the night,' for her childbearing was signaled by a star which brought night from afar, that is, brought the Magi from the East" (Sermon 223D, 2).

Mary's cooperation in redemption makes her the spiritual mother of Christians. She is "spiritual mother, not of our head, that is, the Savior himself . . . but certainly of us, his members, for by her love she cooperated in the birth of the Church of the faithful, who are the members of that head" (*Holy Virginity* 6).

Mary's relationship to the Church occupies an important place in Augustinian theology. The Church, like Mary, is a virgin, and this not only in that chosen portion of her members who have followed the special calling of virginity, but in all Christians, by reason of "the integrity of their faith, their hope, and their charity" (Sermon 188, 4). Christ himself makes the Church a virgin "by rescuing it from fornication with demons" (Sermon 192, 2). Like Mary, the Church combines virginal purity with maternal fruitfulness: "Mary gave birth to your head; the Church gave birth to you. Indeed, the Church is both mother and virgin: mother through the fruitfulness of love, virgin through the integrity of faith and piety" (Sermon 192, 2).

The author of this marvelous union of excellences is Christ himself, "most beautiful of the children of men (Psalm 44 [45]: 3), son of holy Mary, and spouse of holy Church, whom he has made like his own mother by making her our mother and yet at the same time preserving her as a virgin for himself. . . . The Church, then, like Mary, possesses perpetual integrity and uncorrupted fruitfulness" (Sermon 195, 2; see also Sermon 213, 7; *Handbook* 34, 10).

As the last of these passages shows, the relationship of Mary to the Church is not based simply on analogies between properties and functions; it is a vital relationship that reaches to the very center of the mystery of the incarnation and redemption, since in the person of Christ the womb of Mary also gave birth to the Church: "There [in Mary's womb] the only-begotten Son of God deigned to unite human nature with himself, so that he might also unite the spotless Church to himself, the spotless head" (Sermon 191, 2). The angel's announcement, says Augustine, signified that the Church was to be born of the Holy Spirit and the Virgin Mary (Sermon 215, 4).

Another aspect of Mary's role in the work of redemption is to be seen in the law of compensation, according to which she is the woman who repairs the damage woman had done by sinning. This law finds expression in the parallel, so familiar to early tradition, between Eve and Mary. "In order to deceive the man, the poison was administered to him by a woman's hand; in the restoration of man salvation was won by means of a woman. By giving birth to Christ woman made up for the sin of having deceived man" (Sermon 51, 3). "A woman brought us to death; a woman has brought forth life for our sake" (Sermon 184, 2). "Through a woman we were destroyed; through a woman salvation was restored to us" (Sermon 289, 2). "Through woman, death; through woman, life" (Sermon 232, 3; see also *The Christian Combat* 24). In this way "the grace of Christ overcame the cunning of the serpent" (Sermon 190, 2); and woman, whom sin had brought low, was rehabilitated by the childbearing of Mary (in addition to the passages already cited, see Sermon 72A, 4).

Holiness

Since I am expounding the thought of Saint Augustine, Mary's holiness, too, must be linked to her role in the history of salvation. This is because Augustine persistently views this holiness as a paradigm, an example.

Mary's holiness

Augustine sometimes speaks of Mary's holiness in its totality, sometimes of the individual virtues that make it up. When speaking of it in its totality, he may view it either negatively or positively.

Augustine proclaims Mary's holiness in negative terms (that is, holiness as absence of sin) in the following well-known passage: "I make exception of the holy virgin Mary, for the Lord's honor requires me to leave her completely out of the picture as far as sin is concerned. Can we even imagine what an extraordinary abundance of grace was bestowed on her for a complete conquest of sin, because she was to conceive and bring forth him who was certainly without sin?" (*Nature and Grace* 42). This text also gives the reason and source of Mary's holiness: her vocation as mother of Jesus, the Holy One beyond compare.

Are we to understand these words as meaning that Mary was also free of original sin? The statement is certainly a strong one and gives no hint of any limitation, so that as it stands it excludes any and every sin. To attribute original sin to Mary would, it seems, introduce an exception which the text as formulated cannot allow. And many scholars in fact interpret it as asserting Mary's freedom even from original sin.

This interpretation proves problematic, however, when we look, first, at the many passages in Augustine's writings which speak of the law of original sin as universal and admitting but one exception: Jesus, the Word made flesh, and, second, at the argument which Augustine the theologian gives for this universality and single exception. He explains original sin as the effect of the concupiscence that accompanies the act of procreation; and since Jesus alone was conceived without the presence of concupiscence, he alone was free from original sin.

Augustine expounds this view in *Marriage and Desire* 2, 5, 15, where he appeals to the authority of Saint Ambrose. In *Answer to Julian* 5, 15, 52 he asserts that with the exception of the flesh of Christ "all other human flesh is sinful flesh" and that "this concupiscence, the action of which Christ would not allow in his own conception, was the cause of the spread of evil throughout the human race." He then adds that "although the body of Mary had its own origin in concupiscence, it did not in turn conceive by the power of concupiscence." It does not seem possible to reconcile the freedom of Mary from original sin with a thesis set forth in such a clear and unqualified way.

There is more. Augustine cites the accusation which Julian, a Pelagian, brings against Catholics: "He [Jovinian] denied the virginity of Mary because she bore a child; you place her under the power of the devil by reason of her own birth." If Augustine really regarded Mary as an exception to the law of original sin, this would certainly have been the place to say so in refutation of the Pelagian objection. Here in fact is his answer: "We do not leave Mary in the devil's power by reason of her birth, because that result is eliminated by the grace of rebirth." Thus not only does he say nothing of Mary being exempt from original sin, but he even supposes that she did contract it, since she required a "rebirth."

The passage continues with Augustine rebuking the Pelagians, who denied original sin, for placing the holy flesh produced by the Virgin (the flesh of Christ) on the same level as "the flesh of other human beings and making no distinction between the likeness of sinful flesh (Romans 8:3) and sinful flesh itself." He then asserts once again the universal law to which the conception of Mary herself would seem inevitably to be subject (*Unfinished Work in Answer to Julian* 4, 122; see also *ibid.*, 6, 22; *The Literal Meaning of Genesis* 10, 35).

Must we therefore admit a contradiction between the passages just cited and the one in *Nature and Grace,* which seems to exclude all sin whatsoever from Mary? The answer is No, because in the latter passage Augustine is speaking of actual sins, as the context makes clear. At the same time, however, Augustine's uncompromising assertion seems to reflect a conviction deeply rooted in the Christian consciousness, that there can be no possible connection between the Mother of the Redeemer and sin. Furthermore, the reasons which Augustine gives for his statement, namely, the honor and absolute holiness of the Son ("propter honorem Domini" and "quae concipere ac parere meruit, quem constat nullum habuisse peccatum"), seem to allow no possible exception, even for original sin.

Perhaps the divergent views of Augustine can be explained in this way: when he excludes any and every stain of sin from Mary he is echoing the conscious tradition of the Church, a tradition which needs no special theological development, being based on a fittingness or appropriateness (convenientia) that seems obvious in view of the relationship between Mary and Jesus. On the other hand, when the demands of anti-Pelagian controversy require him to demonstrate the universality of original sin, he sees no way of excepting Mary; but his inability to exempt her is due to his own explanation of original sin, which (he says) is communicated by way of the concupiscence inherent in sexual intercourse. I hardly need point out that the weakness of this thesis is enough to undermine the consequence it implies for Mary.

I call attention, finally, to a short passage which, however, does not seem to have original sin in mind: "For, to put it briefly, Mary, being descended from Adam, died because of sin; Adam himself died because of sin; and the flesh which the Lord took from Mary died in order to destroy sin" (*Expositions of the Psalms* 34, 3: "Maria ex Adam mortua propter peccatum, Adam mortuus propter peccatum, et caro Domini ex Maria mortua est propter delenda peccata"). Even if we agree with the Louvain and Maurist editors in accepting this reading, which is that of the majority of the manuscripts (some of these, perhaps for doctrinal reasons, do not mention Mary's death), the context makes it possible, without forcing the text, to explain it as referring to physical death, which is the effect of the first sin, and therefore as providing no basis for arguing to the presence of sin in Mary.

Augustine also affirms the holiness of Mary in positive terms. Thus, after speaking of her superiority to other holy spouses "as far as the integrity of the flesh is concerned," he adds: "As for the other merits of Mary, who can be ignorant of them?" (*The Excellence of Marriage* 35).

Mary's holiness is the result of the grace which God poured out upon her in view of her mission. This principle emerges from the passages in which Augustine speaks of the angel's greeting: "Hail, full of grace." He does not devote special exegetical attention to the words, but on the other hand neither does he regard them as a conventional greeting (Sermon 291, 6; see also Sermon 290, 6; 219, 4; *Expositions of the Psalms* 67, 21; *The Predestination of the Saints* 30).

Mary's virtues

Augustine proclaims Mary's holiness chiefly by concentrating on the individual virtues which shone forth so brightly in the various episodes of her life.

First place belongs to *faith*, a virtue which is to the fore in the mystery of the Annunciation: "The angel announces, the virgin listens, believes, and conceives. Faith is in her soul, Christ in her womb" (Sermon 196, 1; see also Sermon 214, 6; Sermon 229P; *Handbook* 34, 10; *The Merits and Forgiveness of*

Sins 2, 38). The question which Mary asks of the angel: *How can this be, since I do not know any man?* (Luke 1:34), does not indicate either doubt or distrust (as does the similar question of Zechariah in Luke 1:18), but only a firm commitment to virginity (Sermon 215, 3). Precisely because her faith is complete she will retain her bodily integrity as well (Sermon 291, 5). Mary is "full of faith" (Sermon 290, 6). Her faith gives her an even greater claim to greatness than does her motherhood itself: "Mary was therefore more blessed in accepting faith in Christ than in conceiving the flesh of Christ" (*Holy Virginity* 3).

Faith kindled *love* in Mary's soul. Her holy conception of Christ took place "in the Virgin's womb, not amid the heat of fleshly desire but amid the fervor of a love inspired by faith" (Sermon 214, 6).

Mary's *humility* is clear from the words she speaks to Jesus in the temple: "Your father and I have been looking for you anxiously" (Luke 2:48). "She had been given the privilege of bearing the Son of the Most High, and she was very humble; she did not put herself ahead of her husband, even in the order in which she named him, for she said, not "I and your father," but "your father and I." It was Jesus who taught her humility: "The humble Christ would not have taught his mother to be proud" (Sermon 51, 18).

Faith and love, humility and obedience shine out above all in the devotion with which Mary listens to the word of God and does his will. This devotion is suggested especially by the gospel story of Mary and the "brothers" of Jesus seeking him out and by the answer her Son gives (Matthew 12:46-50). "To Mary, the Mother of Christ, belongs the greater blessedness, according to his words which were cited above: *Whoever does the will of my heavenly Father is my brother and sister and mother*" (*Holy Virginity* 5).

In this passage and elsewhere Augustine also mentions the answer which Jesus gives to the acclamation of an anonymous woman of the people: *Blessed is the womb that bore you!* In the words of Jesus: *Rather, blessed are they who hear the word of God and keep it* (Luke 11:27f.). Augustine sees new praise of Mary: "What he meant was: 'Even my mother, whom you are calling blessed, is blessed because she keeps the word of God. She is blessed not because the Word became flesh in her and dwelt among us (John 1:14), but because she keeps the very Word of God by whom she was made and who became a human being in her" (*Homilies on the Gospel of John* 10, 3).

Augustine extols the spotless chastity of Mary when, in passages already cited, he proclaims her complete and perpetual virginity. He likes to emphasize this purity by asserting the absence of any and every trace of sin in the conception of Jesus (*The Literal Meaning of Genesis* 10, 18, 32; Sermon 229P; *Handbook* 34, 10; *The Merits and Forgiveness of Sins* 2, 38; *Marriage and Desire* 1, 13).

Mary's Holiness as Example to the Church

A creature endowed with so radiant a holiness inevitably occupies an incomparable position in the economy of salvation and is destined by her entire being to be a luminous example to the Church. This is a familiar idea to Augustine, who describes various facets of this exemplarity.

Model of Virgins

Augustine takes over for his own use the picture which Saint Ambrose had so carefully and lovingly drawn of Mary as a child (Augustine also regards it as a model of an ornate yet restrained oratorical style). He offers it to consecrated virgins for their imitation (*Christian Instruction* 4, 21). He emphasizes, above all else, Mary's complete chastity, which these virgins have chosen to imitate: "Therefore she in whose footsteps you are following remained a virgin after conceiving her child without the aid of a man and after bringing him to birth. Imitate her as far as you can," that is, not only in virginity but in a fruitfulness of the spirit (Sermon 194, 4). He exclaims, "Rejoice, virgins of Christ, for your companion is Christ's own mother!" and he exhorts them once again to imitate Mary by the spiritual fruitfulness that is the flower of virginity: "Conceive him [Christ] by faith and bring him to birth by your works, in order that what Mary's womb did for the flesh of Christ, your hearts may do for the law of Christ" (Sermon 192, 2).

In the divine plan, the vow by which Mary consecrated her virginity was to serve as an example and show forth a new ideal of holiness: "God could have simply ordered her to remain a virgin on the grounds that the Son of God had taken the form of a slave within her (Philippians 2:7) by an appropriate miracle. She was meant however to serve in the future as a model for holy virgins. In order therefore that Christians might not think that she alone ought to remain a virgin because she had conceived without human assistance, she consecrated her virginity to God by a vow." Virgins can, like Mary, be mothers of Christ by doing the will of his Father (Holy Virginity 4-5; see also Sermon 343, 4).

Model of Spouses

Mary was truly the spouse of Joseph, and she is therefore proposed to all married people as a model. I noted earlier how humility characterized her relations with Joseph (Sermon 51, 18). Her marriage to Joseph did not indeed involve bodily union, but it did involve the far closer union of souls. God arranged things in this manner so that Christian spouses might realize that "the more they learn to imitate the parents of

Christ, the closer will be their union with the members of Christ" (*Answer to Faustus* 23, 8). Thus, while never tiring of exalting Mary's ineffable privilege of virginity combined with motherhood, Augustine sees in her transcendent vocation an exhortation to those Christians who are called to marriage: Let them, like Mary, aim at what is noblest and most exalted in that state!

Model for All the Faithful

Finally, Mary is proposed as a marvelous model of holiness for all the faithful, no matter what their state of life may be. All Christians can become like the Virgin Mary because the Apostle's words are addressed to all of them: *I betrothed you to Christ to present you as a pure bride to her one husband* (2 Corinthians 11:2). This mystical virginity of the Church as a whole consists in "the integrity of faith, hope, and charity" (Sermon 188, 4). How can all the faithful imitate Mary as Mother and virgin? "Do in the depths of your heart what you marvel at in her flesh. Those who believe with their hearts and are justified conceive Christ; those who confess him with their mouths and are saved (Romans 10:10) give birth to Christ. Let your souls, then, be abundantly fruitful and persevere in virginity" (Sermon 191, 4). All the faithful, like Mary, can become mothers of Jesus by doing the will of his Father (*Holy Virginity* 5).

Conclusion

In an attempt at a concluding summary of Augustine's thought on Mary I shall distinguish between those points that emerge clearly from his writings, those that appear in passing, as it were, and those later acquisitions of dogma or theology that do not appear at all.

To be noted in the first group are: a) the real, corporeal maternity of Mary, which Augustine insistently proclaims in opposition to Manichean docetism; b) her perpetual and complete virginity before, during, and after the birth of Christ; this he asserts and defends against Helvidius and Jovinian; c) the unique role of Mary in the economy of redemption; here he emphasizes the contrast with sinful Eve and the relationship to Christ that assimilates and vitally unites Mary and the Church; d) her sublime holiness, which makes her a model for all the faithful.

Deserving of attention in the second group are: a) the divine maternity; Augustine mentions it only briefly, but he asserts (or supposes) the theological principle on which the development of this dogma was to be based; b) Mary's mediatorial function; the seeds of this doctrine are present in the role which he assigns to her in the economy of salvation.

In the third category I must place (for reasons given earlier) the dogma of the Immaculate Conception. This dogma is implicit in the traditional doctrine of Mary's sinlessness, which Augustine rather clearly echoes. At the same time, however, it is irreconcilable with his interpretation of original sin.

As far as the bodily assumption of Mary is concerned: Augustine is silent about it in the passage in which he says that Mary died because of sin, even though a reference to her resurrection and assumption would have appropriately complemented the thought he is setting forth there. We may choose to think that his silence is due to ignorance of the doctrine. But in this same passage he makes no reference to the resurrection of Jesus, which would have been no less appropriate in the context. I conclude, therefore, that his silence proves nothing either way about whether he knew the dogma of the Assumption.

Toward the Council of Ephesus
Mary, Mother of God

The words of Mary to the angel Gabriel were echoed from century to century and were captured in various ways by writers and defenders of the faith. As with most things momentum played a vital role in Mary's yes or fiat.

In the first few centuries the role of Mary in salvific history was written about in a discreet way, the same way that she passed her life and death, in the shadows.

Early writers saw Mary as virgin, the specific sign of the incarnation of the Son of God. Her obedience, her yes, had opened the door for the coming of God into our world.

In the fifth century questions begin to arise about the Mother of Jesus so the writers begin to defend her purest title: Mother of God.

Saint Ignatius of Antioch *(d.107), bishop and martyr, wrote seven major letters of instruction while under persecution. Ignatius did not separate the cross from the virgin birth; the cross and the virgin birth are scandal and mystery combined which defy the wisdom of humanity and the intelligence of Satan, the prince of this world.*

I offer up my life as a poor substitute for the cross, which is a stumbling block to those who have no faith, but to us salvation and eternal life. Where is the wise person? Where is the philosopher? Where is the boasting of the so-called men and women of prudence? For our God Jesus Christ was, according to God's dispensation, the fruit of Mary's womb, of the seed of David; he was born and baptized in order that he might make the water holy by his passion.

The maidenhood of Mary and her childbearing and also the death of the Lord were hidden from the prince of this world — three resounding mysteries wrought in the silence of God. How, then, did he appear in time? A star, brighter than all other stars, shone in the sky, and its brightness was ineffable and the novelty of it caused astonishment. And the rest of the stars, along with the sun and moon, formed a choir about the star, but the light of the star by itself outshone all the rest. It was a puzzle to know the origin of this novelty unlike anything else. Thereupon all magic was dissolved, every bond of malice disappeared, ignorance was destroyed, the ancient kingdom was ruined, when God appeared in the form of man to give newness of eternal life.

To the Ephesians 18-19

*The **Odes of Solomon** (second century) is a very early text which could even predate Saint Ignatius. The text is from the Jewish tradition, most likely from a convert who is reflecting on the joyful mysteries in Luke's gospel.*

The Spirit spread his wings
over the Virgin's womb.
She conceived and gave birth.
And she became a virginal mother by great mercy.
She conceived and gave birth to a son without pain,
and there was a purpose for this.
She did not ask for a midwife to aid her,
because God saw to her delivery.
Like a human being,
she gave birth according to the will of God.
Manifestly she gave birth.
With great power she acquired him.
With thanksgiving she loved him.
With kindness she guarded him.
With grandeur she manifested him.
Alleluia!

Ode 19, 6-11

Justin the Martyr (110-165), a layman, was a professor of philosophy and wrote a famous treatise on Christianity. He had the courage to defend the virginal conception revealed in the scriptures even in the midst of conflict with pagans and Jews.

Christ is born of the Virgin, in order that the disobedience caused by the serpent might be destroyed in the same manner in which it had originated. For Eve, an undefiled virgin, conceived the word of the serpent and brought forth disobedience and death. But the Virgin Mary, filled with faith and joy, when the angel Gabriel announced to her the good tidings that the Spirit of the Lord would come upon her and the power of the Most High would overshadow her, and therefore the Holy One born of her would be the Son of God, answered:

Be it done unto me according to your word.

And indeed, she gave birth to him, concerning whom we have shown so many passages of scripture were written, and by whom God destroys both the serpent and those angels and people who have become like the serpent, but frees from death those who repent of their sins and believe in Christ.

Dialogue with Trypho 100-101

Saint Irenaeus (c.140-201), born and educated in Asia Minor, became bishop of Lyons (France). In this passage he clearly states Mary's role in the mystery of the incarnation and in the work of salvation. As the centuries pass, the role of the new Eve will be understood more clearly.

The Lord came visibly to his own domain and was sustained by his own creation which he himself sustains in being. By his obedience upon a tree he reversed the disobedience shown because of another tree. The seduction to which the betrothed virgin Eve had miserably fallen victim was remedied by the truth happily announced by the angel to Mary, another betrothed virgin.

As Eve, seduced by an angel, turned away from God by disobedience to his word, so Mary, receiving the good news from an angel, bore God in her womb in obedience to his word; and as Eve had been led to disobey God, so Mary was persuaded to obey him. Thus the Virgin Mary became the advocate of the virgin Eve.

Origen (185-253) *was one of the most prolific writers of the early Christian era. In this passage he reflects on Mary as she is venerated from age to age.*

And his mercy is from generation to generation. The mercy of God is not on one generation only, but reaches for ever *from generation unto generation to those who fear him.*

John was not filled with the Holy Spirit until she came who carried Christ in her womb. But then he was both filled with the Holy Spirit and leapt for joy, and made his mother to share with him. And Elizabeth cried out prophetically on account of him whom she bore an infant in her womb, and said to the Virgin: *Blessed are you among women.* For of so great a grace no other woman was ever partaker, nor can be: since one only is the divine conception; one alone the divine birth; one alone is she who gave birth to him who is God and man. Why then do you first salute me? Am I then she who bears the savior? It behooved me to come to you, for you are above all other women blessed: you, my Lady, who bears the undoing of the curse. She speaks in accordance with the son. For John spoke of himself as unworthy to come before Christ, and she calls herself unworthy of the Virgin's presence. What such great good, she says, has been done by me, *that the mother of my Lord should come to me?* And she calls her who was yet a virgin, mother, prophetically by her word anticipating the event, and names the Savior the fruit of her womb, because he was not to be from man, but from Mary alone.

Homily 8 on Luke

Saint Ephrem (306-373), *a deacon, retired to a cave near Edessa and lived an austere life. He preached to the people and composed popular ballads and poetry on religious themes. In his poetry he puts Greek speculation on the Divine entering the world in mystical, biblical, and liturgical language and highlights Mary's role as mother and virgin.*

Look upon Mary, my beloved,
how, when Gabriel entered in to her
and she spoke with him words of enquiry:
"How shall these things be?",
and the minister of the Spirit gave reply to Mary
and said: "It is easy for God,
all things are simple for him" —
how she held it true when she heard, and said:
"Behold, his handmaid am I."
Therefore he came down, in a manner he knows,
he stirred and came in a way without her perceiving,
she received him, suffering nothing.
He was in her womb like a babe,
yet the whole world was full of him.
Of his love he came down to renew
the image of Adam grown old.
Therefore, when you hear of the birth of God,
remain in silence;
let the word of Gabriel be depicted in your mind,
for there is nothing that is hard
for that glorious majesty,
which for our sakes leaned down,
and for our sakes was revealed,
for it leaned down toward us,
and among us was born, from one of us.

Mary has become for us the heaven that bears God,
for in her the exalted Godhead
has descended and dwelt;
in her it has grown small, to make us great,
– but its nature does not diminish;
in her it has woven us a garment
that shall be for our salvation.
In her the words of the prophets and the just
are all contained;
from her the luminous One has shone forth
and dispelled the darkness of paganism.
The titles of Mary are many
and it is right that I should use them:
she is the palace where dwells
the mighty King of Kings;
not as he entered her did he leave her,
for from her he put on a body and came forth.
Again, she is the new heaven,
in which there dwells the King of Kings;
he shone out in her and came forth into creation,
formed and clothed in her features.
She is the stem of the cluster of grapes,
she gave forth fruit beyond nature's means,
and he, though his nature bore no resemblance to her,
put on her hue and came forth from her.
She is the spring,
whence flowed living water for the thirsty,
and those who have tasted its draught
give forth fruit a hundred fold.

Homily on the Nativity

48

Saint Ambrose (339-397) *after a military career was elected bishop of Milan and soon became known as the most eloquent preacher of his day. Saint Augustine was attracted to his preaching and was baptized by Saint Ambrose. In this passage he shows how God prepared Saint John the Baptist and our Lady for their vocation, and then applies Elizabeth's words to each individual believer.*

When announcing the mystery to the Virgin Mary, the angel helped her to believe by giving her a precedent. He told her of the motherhood of a woman who was old and barren, for this demonstrated God's power to do whatever he wills.

At this news Mary set out for the hill country, not because she doubted the angel's word, felt uncertain of the message, or questioned the precedent, but because of her own eager desire. She was anxious to be of service and joy impelled her to make haste. Filled with God, where could she hasten but to the heights? The Holy Spirit does not proceed by slow, laborious efforts. Quickly, too, the blessings of her coming and of the Lord's presence were revealed: *As soon as Elizabeth heard Mary's greeting the child leapt in her womb and she was filled with the Holy Spirit.*

Notice the choice of words and the meaning of each one. Elizabeth was the first to hear Mary's voice, but John was the first to be aware of grace. She heard with the ears of the body; he leapt for joy because of the mystery. She was aware of Mary's presence, he of the Lord's.

The woman perceived the presence of a woman, the child that of a child. The women spoke of God's grace while the children gave effect to it within them, revealing to their mothers the mystery of love, and by a double miracle the mothers prophesied under the inspiration of their sons.

The child leapt in the womb; the mother was filled with the Holy Spirit. The mother was not filled before her son, but once he had been filled with the Holy Spirit, he filled his mother too. John leapt for joy and so did the spirit of Mary. When John leapt Elizabeth was filled with the Holy Spirit, but we do not learn that Mary was then filled with the Holy Spirit, only that her spirit rejoiced. Her son, who is beyond our understanding, was active in his mother in a way beyond our understanding. Elizabeth was filled with the Holy Spirit after conceiving a son; Mary was filled before. *You are blessed,* said Elizabeth, *because you have believed.*

You too are blessed because you have heard and believed. The soul of every believer conceives and brings forth the Word of God and recognizes his works. Let Mary's soul be in each of you to glorify the Lord. Let her spirit be in each of you to rejoice in the Lord. Christ has only one mother in the flesh, but we all bring forth Christ by faith. Every soul free from the contamination of sin and inviolate in its purity can receive the Word of God.

Commentary on Luke's Gospel 2, 19ff

Saint John Chrysostom (347-407) was a prolific writer as well as archbishop of Constantinople. He died in exile. The golden-mouthed preacher, as he was known, breaks into lyrical song in praise of God's wonderful work of salvation. He then makes an act of faith in the mystery of the incarnation.

Christ who was inexpressibly begotten by the Father is marvelously brought forth by a virgin for my sake. In his own nature he was begotten by the Father before all ages in a manner known only to the One who engendered him; outside his own nature he is today brought forth anew in a manner known only to the Holy Spirit's grace. His birth on high was real; his birth here below is real. He was truly begotten as God from God and he is truly brought forth by the Virgin as man. In heaven he is the Father's only Son, Unique from the Unique; on earth he is the Virgin's only Son, unique from her who is also unique.

I know a virgin bore a son today and I believe that God begot a Son before time was, but the manner in which this happened I have learned to venerate in silence and I have been taught not inquisitively to inquire by busy reasoning. Where God is concerned we should not regard the order of nature, but believe in the power of the One at work therein.

Homily on Christ's Birth

*Praising Mary as both virgin and mother, and the most exalted of all creatures, this **Writer of the Fifth Century** exhorts his hearers to believe the paradoxes of our faith on the authority of the Fathers of the Church.*

May we all receive the benefit of having recourse to the holy Virgin and Mother of God. Those of you who are now virgins should be devoted to the Mother of the Lord, because it is she who procures for you this fair and incorruptible possession. Truly great is the wonder of the Virgin. What can ever be found greater than all that exists? She alone has appeared wider than earth and heaven. Who is holier than she? She is unsurpassed by our ancestors, by the prophets, apostles, or martyrs, by these patriarchs or the Fathers, by the angels, thrones, dominions, seraphim, or cherubim, or by any other created thing visible or invisible. She is a servant and the Mother of God, a virgin and a mother. And let no one be doubtful and ask how she can be a servant and the Mother of God, or how she can be a virgin and a mother. Accept with faith and do not doubt teachings that have been examined and approved by the Fathers. Instead, stand in awe and believe without question, or rather, without being inquisitive. If your beliefs correspond to your own ideas, perceive your danger. But if you believe the word that is preached, it is no longer you who must render an account but the bishop.

Believe what we say about the Virgin, and do not hesitate to confess her to be both servant and Mother of God, both virgin and mother.

Mary is a servant as the creature of him who was born of her; she is the Mother of God inasmuch as of her God was born in human flesh. She is a virgin because she did not conceive from the seed of man; she is a mother because she gave birth and became the mother of him who before all eternity was begotten of the Father.

She is therefore the mother of the Lord of angels and our mother; from her the Son of God received the human body in which he consented to be crucified. Do you desire to know how far the Virgin surpasses the powers of heaven? Give me your attention then. They veil their faces as they hover in fear and trembling, but she offers the human race to God, and through her we receive the forgiveness of our sins. She bore him whom the angels glorified when they came with reverence to be present at his birth. *Glory to God in the highest*, they sang, *and peace to his people on earth.*

Rejoice, then, mother and heaven, maiden and cloud, virgin and throne, the boast and foundation of our Church. Plead earnestly for us that through you we may obtain mercy on the Day of Judgment and attain the good things reserved for those who love God, through the grace and love of our Lord Jesus Christ, to whom with the Father and the Holy Spirit be glory, power, and honor now and for ever and for all eternity. Amen.

Homily attributed to Saint John Chrysostom

Saint Augustine (354-430), *after his conversion to Christianity, established religious communities in Northern Africa and became bishop of Hippo. His writings have shaped Christian thought for centuries. In this text, preached in 412 or 416, we have one of the most beautiful reflections on Mary's reply or fiat to the angel.*

The holy one to be born of you shall be called Son of God. Who are you that you should give birth to him? How did you deserve it? Why is the privilege yours? Why did your maker become a creature in you? Why is this great blessing yours? You are holy, you are a virgin, you have taken a vow. But if you have merited much, much too has been freely given to you. For how could you have merited that your maker should take form in you? that the Word of God by whom you were made and by whom even heaven and earth and all things were made, should take flesh in you, making flesh his own without losing his divinity? The Word is joined to flesh; the Word is married to flesh, and your womb is the bridal chamber of that great marriage.

Why should so great a privilege be yours? But surely I am impudent to question a virgin thus, unmannerly to besiege thus her chaste ears? Yet I see this modest virgin answering and reminding me: "You ask why this privilege is mine? I shrink from telling you of the good found in me; hear, instead, the angel's greeting and recognize in me him who is your salvation. Believe in him in whom I have put my trust. Why, you ask, is this privilege mine? Let the angel answer!"

"Tell me, angel, why was this privilege given to Mary?"

"I gave the explanation when I said: *Hail, full of grace.*"

Sermon 291, 6

Augustine, like Irenaeus, compares Eve and Mary, but unlike Irenaeus he sees Eve's role in a positive vein. Also in this passage he extols Mary's role. Later in the sixteenth and seventeenth centuries the "slaves of Mary" theme would refer to this concept "through Mary."

Unless Adam had fallen in the body, Christ would not have raised us up to this new life in the spirit. O great and wondrous mystery! O ordering hidden from the wicked and shown forth to the faithful! The immortal One builds up mortal man, and mortality gives birth to immortality. The incorporeal God is contained by the earth, man is encompassed with heaven. God is made man, and as man he is believed in as God. All this is the result of Eve's action which is remedied through Mary. Happy Eve therefore, through whom death arose; happier still Mary the instrument of purification. Happy Eve as the mother of people; happier Mary, the Mother of our Lord. Thus one is more blessed than the other. Both indeed are glorious, for Christ would not have made the blessedness of Mary if he had not first designed the first Eve, of whom Mary herself was born. Nor would he have come to his people unless she had first sinned in this world. Eve is the mother of the human race; Mary the author of their salvation. Eve formed us; Mary strengthened us. We multiply every day through Eve; we reign eternally through Mary: we are borne down to earth by Eve, and are raised to heaven through Mary.

Sermon attributed to Augustine

Ephesus and Chalcedon

In solemn council at Ephesus Mary's yes and her role in salvation history as Mother of God was solemnly proclaimed for ages to come.

> If anyone does not confess that God is truly Emmanuel, and that on this account the holy Virgin is the Mother of God (for according to the flesh she gave birth to the Word of God become flesh by birth), let him be anathema.

The place of Mary is found within the framework of the mystery of the incarnation.

In 451 the Fourth Ecumenical Council was celebrated at Chalcedon. Although it concentrated on the two natures and one person of Christ, the Council likewise acknowledged Mary's role:

> Following the holy fathers we all teach that with one accord we confess one and the same Son, our Lord Jesus Christ, the same perfect in human nature, truly God and the same with a rational soul and a body, truly man, consubstantial with the Father according to divinity, and consubstantial with us according to human nature, like unto us in all things except sin (Hebrews 4:15); indeed born of the Father before the ages according to divine nature, but in the last days the same born of the virgin Mary, Mother of God according to human nature.

After the councils of Ephesus and Chalcedon writers continued to emphasize Mary's role in salvation history and were very emphatic about her place in Christian belief. This continued until the ninth century.

*This is the most famous marian homily of antiquity. It was delivered by **Saint Cyril of Alexandria** (d. 444) in the Church of Saint Mary at Ephesus between 23 and 27 June 431, while the Third Ecumenical Council was in session there. This council, at which Cyril presided as papal legate, condemned Nestorius, and solemnly recognized Mary's title of Theotokos, Mother of God.*

Mary, Mother of God, we salute you. Precious vessel, worthy of the whole world's reverence, you are an ever-shining light, the crown of virginity, the symbol of orthodoxy, an indestructible temple, the place that held him whom no place can contain, mother and virgin. Because of you the holy gospels could say: *Blessed is he who comes in the name of the Lord.*

We salute you, for in your holy womb he, who is beyond all limitation, was confined. Because of you the holy Trinity is glorified and adored; the cross is called precious and is venerated throughout the world; the heavens exult; the angels and archangels make merry; demons are put to flight; the devil, that tempter, is thrust down from heaven; the fallen race of humanity is taken up on high; all creatures possessed by the madness of idolatry have attained knowledge of the truth; believers receive holy baptism; the oil of gladness is poured out; the Church is established throughout the world; pagans are brought to repentance.

What more is there to say? Because of you the light of the only-begotten Son of God has shone upon those who sat in darkness and in the shadow of death; prophets pronounced the word of God; the apostles preached salvation to the Gentiles; the dead are raised to life, and kings rule by the power of the holy Trinity.

Who can put Mary's high honor into words? She is both mother and virgin. I am overwhelmed by the wonder of this miracle. Of course no one could be prevented from living in the house he had built for himself, yet who would invite mockery by asking his own servant to become his mother?

Behold then the joy of the whole universe. Let the union of God and man in the Son of the Virgin Mary fill us with awe and adoration. Let us fear and worship the undivided Trinity as we sing the praise of the ever-virgin Mary, the holy temple of God, and of God himself, her Son and spotless Bridegroom. To him be glory for ever and ever. Amen.

Homily 4

Saint Vincent of Lerins (d.450) *became a monk at the abbey of Lerins. He straddles the two councils, Ephesus devoted to Mary, Mother of God, and Chalcedon devoted to Christ, God and man.*

The unity of the person in Christ was formed and completed, not after the birth from the Virgin, but in the very womb of the Virgin. We must therefore take utmost care to be precise in our confession, so as to say that Christ is not merely one, but that he always has been one. It were, indeed, an intolerable blasphemy to assert that, although you admit his now being one, you contend that he once was not one but two — one after baptism but two at the time of his birth.

Through this unity of person it also becomes perfectly clear — by reason of a similar mystery — that it is most truly Catholic to believe (and most impious to deny) that the Word of God himself was born from the Virgin even as the flesh of the Word was born from an immaculate mother.

May God forbid that anyone should attempt to defraud holy Mary of her privileges of divine grace and her special glory. For by a unique favor of our Lord and God she is confessed to be the most true and most blessed Mother of God (*theotokos*). Holy Mary is the Mother of God because in her sacred womb was accomplished the mystery that, by reason of a certain singular and unique unity of person, even as the Word is flesh in flesh, so the man is God in God.

The Commonitories 15

Saint Peter Chrysologus *(400-450), bishop of Ravenna, Italy, was highly esteemed as a preacher and was above all a pastor. In this passage he sees Mary's role in the realm of the divine mystery.*

A virgin conceived, and a virgin brought forth her child. Do not be disturbed at this conception or confused when you hear of this birth. If there is any human shame, her virginity excuses it. What injury is there to modesty when the Deity enters into union with that virginity always dear to himself? Where an angel is the mediator, faith the bridesmaid, chastity the betrothal, virtue the dowry, conscience the judge, God the cause, integrity the conception, virginity the birth, a virgin the mother?

Therefore, let no one judge in a human way what is done in a divine mystery. Let no one try to penetrate this heavenly mystery by earthly reasoning. Let no one treat this novel secret from knowledge of everyday occurrences. Let no one manipulate the work of love into an insult, or run the risk of losing salvation.

Sermon 148

Saint Basil of Seleucia (d.459), *archbishop, tried with his homilies to place the exegesis of his time within the reach of all. In this selection the author sings the praises of the Mother of God. Mary ponders in her heart the mystery of the incarnate Word. She, the mother of Emmanuel, is the cause of our joy.*

Born of the Virgin Mother of God, the Creator and Lord of all shared our human nature, for he has a real body and soul even though he had no part in our misdeeds. *He committed no sin*, says Scripture, *and no falsehood ever came from his mouth.* O holy womb in which God was received, in which the record of our sins was effaced, in which God became man while remaining God! He was carried in the womb, condescending to be born in the same way as we are. Yet when he was received into the arms of his mother he did not leave the bosom of his Father. God is not divided as he carries out his will, but saves the world without suffering any division in himself. When Gabriel came into the presence of the Virgin Mother of God he left heaven behind, but when the Word of God who fills all creation took flesh within her, he was not separated from the adoring hosts of heaven.

Is there any need to enumerate all the prophecies foretelling Christ's birth of the Mother of God? What tongue could worthily hymn her through whom we have received such magnificent blessings? With what flowers of praise could we weave a fitting crown for her from whom sprang the flower of Jesse, who has crowned our race with glory and honor. What gifts could we bring that would be worthy of her of whom the whole world is unworthy? If Paul could say of the other saints that the world was not worthy of them, what can we say of the Mother of God, who outshines all the martyrs even as the sun outshines the stars? O Virgin, well may the angels rejoice in you! Because of you they who long ages ago had banished our race are now sent to our service, and to his joy Gabriel is entrusted with the news of a divine child's conception. *Rejoice, most favored one,* let your face glow with gladness. You are to give birth to the joy of all the world, who will put an end to the age-old curse, destroying the power of death and giving to all the hope of resurrection.

And all these things together with other marvels concerning him the holy mother of the Lord of all creation, the mother in very truth of God, *pondered in her heart,* and her heart was filled with great gladness. She was radiant with joy and amazed when she thought of the majesty of her Son who was also God. As her gaze rested upon that divine child I think she must have been overwhelmed by awe and longing. She was alone conversing with the Alone.

Homily 39, 4-5

Saint Leo the Great (400-461) was elected pope in 440 and thus had a part in the Council of Chalcedon. His many sermons and letters usually highlight Christological teachings and also Mary as the Mother of God. In this passage the pope teaches his people what it means to be born in a new way.

When the devil's malice destroyed us by the poison of his hate, God the almighty and compassionate, whose nature is goodness, whose will is power, whose activity is mercy, immediately, at the very beginning of the world, foretold the remedy his love had prepared for the restoration of us mortals, giving notice to the serpent that the offspring of the woman would come and, by his power, crush its baneful head as it was raised to strike. He referred to Christ who would come in the flesh and be both God and man, and who, being born of a virgin, would condemn by his untainted birth the perverter of human stock.

When the time appointed for the redemption of our race arrived, Jesus Christ, the Son of God, came down from his heavenly throne to this lowly world without departing from his Father's glory, and was born in a new manner, by a new kind of birth. When God was born in the flesh, it was God who begot him, as the archangel testified to the blessed Virgin Mary: *The Holy Spirit will come upon you, and the power of the Most High will overshadow you; and so the holy one who will be born of you will be called the Son of God.*

Christ's birth was different from ours, but his nature was the same. It is contrary to nature's law for a virgin to conceive and give birth and yet remain a virgin, but in this case God's power intervened. Do not consider the status of the mother, but the choice of the child who wished and had the power to be born as a man in this way. The Lord Jesus came to remove our pollution, not to be infected by it; to correct our faults, not to succumb to them. He came to cure all the sickness of our corrupted nature and all the wounds of our defiled souls. He therefore who brought to human bodies the new gift of unsullied integrity had to be born in a new way.

If, then, with faith and religious feeling, you take pride in the title of Christian, value the grace of this reconciliation at its true worth. Once you were cast off, driven from paradise, dying in weary exile. Reduced to dust and ashes, you had no further hope of life, but now through the incarnation of the Word you have the power to return from afar to your Creator, to recognize your Father, to be freed from slavery, and to be raised from the status of a stranger to that of a child.

Christmas Sermon II, 1-2.5

Romanos Melodos (d.555/65), a convert from Judaism, portrays Mary's thought on her fiat in a poetic text. He also has a beautiful rendition of the Way of the Cross.

Knowing this birth to be beyond nature's powers she was afraid and trembled and thought thus within herself:

"What name shall I discover for you, my Son?

If, looking upon you, I call you 'a man,' yet you are above all human beings, for you, only Friend of humankind, preserved my virginity intact!

Shall I call you 'perfect man'? But I know well that your conception was divine, for no human being was ever conceived without union and seed, as you were, Sinless One!

And if I call you 'God,' I marvel to see you entirely like me, for there is nothing in you to distinguish you from human beings, except that you were conceived and born without sin. Should I, then, nurse you or sing your glory?

The event proclaims you to be God who transcends time, even though, only Friend of humankind, you became a human being yourself."

Hymn 14, The Presentation, 3-4

Saint Gregory the Great (540-604), *a Benedictine monk, had a brilliant secular career before entering religious life. He preached to the monks with whom he lived and later as pope he preached to the flock of Rome. While pope he wrote the* Dialogues *which contain lives of the saints. In this passage he shows us that Mary, even in his time, visited her Son's followers.*

I include the story Probus told me about his little sister Musa. One night the Blessed Virgin Mary, Mother of God, appeared to her and showed her other little girls of her own age dressed in white. Though Musa was eager to be with them, she did not dare join their ranks. Noticing this, the Blessed Virgin asked her whether she wished to be with them in her court. Naturally, the little girl said she did. Whereupon, our Blessed Lady commanded her not to do anything silly, as foolish little girls often do; instead, she was to keep from laughing and joking, and to remember at all times that in thirty days she would be one of the little girls in white.

After the vision the girl's character was completely changed. Her astounded parents asked her for an explanation of this sudden change. She told them that the Blessed Virgin had given her special instructions and had set the day on which she was to join her companions in heaven. After the twenty-fifth day she fell sick with a fever. On the thirtieth, as the hour of her death drew near, she saw the Blessed Virgin coming to her with the same train of girls. Our Blessed Lady called to her, and little Musa reverently lowered her eyes as she answered with a clear voice, "I am coming, my noble Lady, I am coming to you."

Dialogue 4, 17-18

Saint Modestus (d.630), *patriarch of Jerusalem, worked for the restoration of Jerusalem as a holy city. In this homily he speaks about Mary's death in light of the one who gave Jesus life.*

When she had successfully completed her voyage through life, the human ship which had carried her God reached the haven of perfect peace beside the helmsman of the world who, with her help, had saved the human race from the flood of godlessness and sin, and given it life. He who gave one law on Sinai, and issued another from Zion, our God himself, sent there to have the ark which he had sanctified brought to him, the ark of which David her ancestor had sung: *Go up, Lord, to your resting place, you and the ark which you have sanctified.*

This ark was not drawn by oxen like the Mosaic ark of old, but guided and guarded by a heavenly army of holy angels. It was not an ark made by hands and plated with gold, but a living ark created by God, wholly luminous with the radiance of the all-holy and life-giving Spirit who had visited her. Within this ark there was no jar of manna, no tablets of the covenant, but instead the bestower of manna and of the promised blessings of eternity, the Lord of the new and the old covenants, who from this ark came into the world as a child and freed those who believe in him from the curse of the law. This ark did not have Aaron's rod within and the glorious Cherubim above, but possessed the incomparably greater glory of being herself the rod of Jesse, and of being overshadowed by the divine, the almighty power of the supremely exalted Father.

Instead of preceding the Hebrew people like the earlier ark, this ark followed God when he appeared on earth in the body received from her. Blessed by angels and humans alike to the glory of him who exalts her above all creatures in heaven and on earth, her holy lips exclaimed: *My soul proclaims the greatness of the Lord, my spirit rejoices in God my Savior.*

In order to shine out clearly, this light-bringing spiritual dawn came to dwell in the radiance of the Sun of Righteousness, in obedience to him who rose by his own power to give light to all creation. Through her the splendor that outshines even the rays of the sun sheds his light upon us in mercy and compassion, stirring up in the souls of believers the desire to imitate as far as they can his divine kindness and goodness. For Christ our God, who from this maiden who remained always a virgin and from the Holy Spirit had clothed himself in a human body possessed of soul and mind, called her to himself and clothed her in immortality, since she was his own flesh and blood. Because she was his most holy Mother, he bestowed on her the highest honor by making her his heir: as the Psalmist sings: *The Queen stands on your right robed in raiment wrought with gold and divers colors.*

The Dormition of Mary 4-5

Saint Ildephonsus (607-677), *monk and abbot, served the church in Spain as archbishop of Toledo. He composed a prayer which echoes the* Sub tuum praesidium *of the third century.*

I ask and beg you, holy Virgin,
that from this Spirit
who brought Jesus to birth in you
I too may receive Jesus.
Let my soul receive him from this Spirit
who caused your flesh to conceive him.

May I love Jesus in this Spirit
in whom you yourself worship him as your Lord
and contemplate him as your Son.

On the Perpetual Virginity of Saint Mary 12

Beginnings of Mary's Immaculate Conception

The writers of the eighth century continue the themes of Ephesus and Chalcedon. Authors begin to depict Mary as a model for others. Writers begin to speak of Mary's immaculate conception.

Saint Germanus (634-733), *patriarch of Constantinople, may be considered one of the first mariologists in the modern sense of the word. Seven of his nine homilies that are preserved give witness to marian doctrine. In the first selection Saint Germanus reflects on Mary's death in the light of her yes in becoming the mother of Jesus. Then follow two prayers to Mary.*

Most truly and with grateful heart I say: You, O Mother of God, are not cut off from us even though you have been removed from our midst. You are not far from this perishable world, you who now live in imperishable life; but on the contrary you draw near to those who call on you, you are found by those who seek you in faith. This is a clear indication of your living, dynamic and continually active spirit and your everlasting body. For how could the dissolution of the body turn into dust and ashes you who freed humankind from the destruction of death through the flesh taken from you by your Son?

Indeed you left the earth to prove that the mystery of the awe-inspiring incarnation did in fact take place. Through your awaiting the natural end of human life, God who was born of you would be believed to have come from you also as perfect man, son of a true mother who was herself subject to the constraints of nature, the decrees of God, and the limitations of an earthly lifetime. For because you had a body like the rest of us, you could not escape death, the lot of all humankind.

The Dormition of the Blessed Mother I

My Lady, hear my pleas, take pity on my groans, and heed my tears, for you alone are my consolation from God, the divine dew that assuages my scorching heat, the drop divinely flowing from my parched heart, the torch that shines brightly in my darkened soul, my guide on my journey, my strength in my weakness, the robe that covers my nakedness, my wealth amid my poverty, the healing for my unhealable wounds. You dry my tears and put an end to my groans and change my misfortunes for the better. You solace me in my sufferings, remove my chains, and give me hope of salvation.

Homily on Mary II

My Lady, my refuge, life, and help, my armor and my boast, my hope and my strength, grant that I may enjoy the ineffable, inconceivable gifts of your Son, your God and our God, in the heavenly kingdom. For I know surely that you have power to do as you will, since you are Mother of the Most High. Therefore, Lady Most Pure, I beg you that I may not be disappointed in my expectations but obtain them, O Spouse of God, who bore him who is the expectation of all: Our Lord Jesus Christ, true God and Master of all things visible and invisible, to whom belongs all glory, honor, and respect, now and always and through endless ages. Amen.

Homily on Mary III

*The following reading by an unknown **Greek author** is taken from a remarkable homily written in the eighth century. It alludes to the queenship of Mary and to Mary as domina or lady.*

After Christ had been born of the Virgin and had accomplished all that pertained to the divine plan concerning his death upon the cross, he said on rising again: *All authority in heaven and on earth has been given to me.* From that time on, then, he was king, and he is proclaimed king of the Christians. This is why we encourage one another at the beginning of our prayers with the cry, "Come, let us worship and fall down before Christ our King." When he appears in his great and manifest second coming he will abide as king for ever, and *his kingdom will have no end.* Moreover, since he who was born of the Virgin is himself king and himself the Lord God, she who bore him is on his account properly and truly declared to be queen and lady and Mother of God.

She stood at your right hand, robed in a gown of gold, with adornment intricately wrought. Just as, being a woman, she was named queen and lady and Mother of God, so also now, standing as queen at the right hand of her most regal Son, she is celebrated in the sacred words of scripture as clothed in the golden gown of incorruptibility. And so as we gaze upon him who is our king and lord and God, and upon her who is queen and lady and the Mother of God.

Annunciation of the Godbearer 13-15

Saint Bede (672-735), *the father of English history, was the most learned individual of his day. In this passage he points to Mary as a model for those who travel toward the kingdom.*

Matthew the evangelist gives us an account of the way in which the eternal Son of God, begotten before the world began, appeared in time as the Son of Man. His description is brief but absolutely true. By tracing the ancestry of our Lord and Savior Jesus Christ through the male line he brings it down from Abraham to Joseph, the husband of Mary. It is indeed fitting in every respect that when God decided to become incarnate for the sake of the whole human race none but a virgin should be his mother, and that, since a virgin was privileged to bring him into the world, she should bear no other son but God.

Behold, a virgin will conceive and bear a son, and he will be called Emmanuel, a name which means God-with-us. And so Mary gave birth to her firstborn son, the child of her own flesh and blood. She brought forth the God who had been born of God before creation began, and who, in his created humanity, rightfully surpassed the whole of creation. As scripture says *she named him Jesus.* Jesus, then, is the name of the Virgin's son. According to the angel's explanation, it means one who is to save his people from their sins.

Homily 5 on the Vigil of Christ's Birth

Saint Andrew of Crete (660-740), *was distinguished as a preacher and writer of hymns, saints' lives, and homilies. He tells us that Mary is the virgin earth of the new creation. Writers now begin to be more explicit about Mary's immaculate conception.*

On the feast of Mary's birth humankind's spotless original nobility recovers the grace of its first emergence from the hands of God, and returns to that state. The degeneration of sin had obscured the charm and beauty of this original nobility. But when the Mother of the supreme Beauty was born, our nature recovered its purity and once again saw itself made in the perfect form that was worthy of God. This refashioning is a restoration, a divinization, an assimiliation to the original state.

Man had originally been formed from undefiled earth, but his nature saw itself deprived of its innate dignity when it was stripped of grace through the fall into disobedience and driven from the land of life. Instead of a paradise of delights it had only a corruptible life to hand down to us as an inheritance, a life followed by death and its consequence: the corruption of the race. So we were all preferring this lower world to life on high. No hope of salvation remained; the state of our nature cried to heaven for help. There was no law which could heal our sickness: neither the natural law nor the written law; neither the flaming speech of the prophets nor their words of reconciliation were of any avail. No one was able to restore human nature; there was nothing which could give it a chance of recovering more or less easily its pristine nobility.

The divine Author of the universe decided to make a new world appear, another world — full of youth and harmony — from which the invading contagion of sin and its companion, death, would be dispelled. A life wholly new, free, and clear would be offered to us: in baptism we were to find a new birth that would be wholly divine.

But how were we to attain to this great gift, so amazing and so worthy of the ways of God? How better than through the manifestation of God in the flesh, through his submission to the laws of our nature, his acceptance of a condition that would be new to him but wholly like ours? And how was this plan to be brought into effect? Was it not fitting that a very pure, spotless virgin should be chosen to serve this mysterious plan, and become pregnant with infinite being, after a mode transcending our natural laws?

And where was this virgin to be found, except in this woman unique above all others, chosen by the Creator of the universe before all generations? Yes, it is she, the Mother of God, Mary of the divine name, whose womb has given the light of day to God incarnate and whom he himself prepared supernaturally as a temple.

The Savior of the human race willed that a new creation and order should replace the old. Just as in the beginning he used virginal, stainless earth for clay out of which to fashion the first Adam, so again to effect his own incarnation he chose, out of all created nature, this utterly pure and stainless Virgin, in place as it were of the original earth.

Sermon 1 on the Nativity of Mary

Saint John Damascene (d.749) did for the Church of the East what Saint Thomas Aquinas did for the Church of the West — a compilation of belief in the true faith. He rejoices in Mary and compares her to a book that originates in the heart of the Father and is written by the Holy Spirit. This passage has a ring of Eastern spirituality concerning the economy of salvation.

O daughter of Adam and Mother of God! Today God the Word, creator of all things, has composed a new book that originates in the heart of the Father and is written by the Holy Spirit, who is the tongue of God. This book was given to literate man who nonetheless did not read it, for Joseph did not in fact know Mary or the meaning of the Mystery itself. O all-holy daughter of Joachim and Anne, you eluded the gaze of the principalities and powers and *the flaming arrows of the Evil One*. You dwelt in the bridal chamber of the Spirit and were kept unsullied that you might become the Bride of God and natural Mother of God! All-holy daughter, you made your appearance in your mother's arms, and you strike terror into the rebellious powers.

Worthy daughter of God, beautiful flower of nature, human being in whom Eve, our first mother, is rehabilitated! By your birth she who fell is now raised up. All-holy daughter, splendor of women! The first Eve was guilty of sin, and death made its entrance through her, because in opposition to our first father she served the serpent. Mary, on the contrary, became the servant of God's will. She deceived the deceitful serpent and brought immortality into the world.

Homily on the Birth of Mary 4-6

Saint Theodore of Studios (759-826), *head of the monastery at Studios, wrote on monastic life and the veneration of images; he is author of many sermons and letters. As noted in this passage, the East begins to speak about the Immaculate Conception of Mary. This passage shows that Mary is the new creation prepared by God to receive the new Adam. The metaphors used by Theodore and other Greek fathers suggest a belief in what the Western Church defines as the Immaculate Conception.*

No creature was ever so holy as the blessed and most admirable Virgin Mary. What is purer than she? What more faultless? So greatly was she loved by God, the supreme and most pure light, that by the coming of the Holy Spirit he united his own substance with hers and came forth from her as a perfect man, although in his own nature there was no alteration or mingling.

How marvelous that in his great love for us God was not ashamed to take his own maidservant as his mother! What condescension! He who is supremely good did not refuse to be called the child of his own creature, for he loved her who was manifestly the fairest of all creatures and took as his own her who was worthier than the powers of heaven.

It is of Mary that the admirable Zechariah speaks when he says: *Sing and rejoice, daughter of Zion, for I am coming to dwell in the midst of you, says the Lord.* And it seems to me that the blessed Joel is referring to her when he cries out: *Do not be afraid, O land; be glad and rejoice, for the Lord has done great things for you.*

Mary is a land. She is the land on which the saintly Moses was ordered to take off his sandals as a symbol of the law which was to be superseded by grace. She is the land on which *he who established the earth on its foundations*, as we sing, was himself established in the flesh by the Spirit. She is the land which without ever being sown nourished him who nourishes all. She is the land on which no thorns of sin ever grew. On the contrary, through the shoot this land produced, sin has been utterly rooted out. She is the land, not cursed like the former land whose crops were full of thorns and thistles, but blessed by the Lord. Blessed is the fruit of the womb of this land, as sacred scripture says!

Rejoice, dwelling place of the Lord, land on which God has walked! Through the incarnation you gave a place to him who in his divinity is beyond any place. Through you he whose nature is simple received a composite human nature; he who is eternal entered time; he who is infinite became finite. Rejoice, dwelling place of God, house shining with divine splendor.

Rejoice, Mary, full of grace. You are called and really are the most gracious of all joys, for from you was born Christ, the eternal joy and the vanquisher of our grief. Rejoice, paradise more blessed than the garden of Eden, paradise in which has sprung up once more every plant of virtue and in which the tree of life has been revealed.

Homily 3 on the Birth of Mary 4-7

Blessed Rabanus Maurus (776-856), *archbishop of Mainz, Germany, was referred to as the "Teacher of Germany," for he did much for the evangelization of that country. In this passage Rabanus sings of Mary's reply to the angel and how her reply changed the world.*

Let our earth rejoice greatly now that it is made glorious by the birth of this great Virgin, by whose own childbearing the nature of creatures was changed and their sin thus wiped away. For in that childbearing the divine sentence of misfortune was rescinded —*In sorrow shall you bring forth children* — because Mary gave birth in the joy of the Lord. Eve mourned, Mary rejoiced. Eve carried tears in her womb, Mary joy, for Eve gave birth to sinners but Mary to a spotless one; moreover she gave birth as a virgin and remained a virgin after childbirth. Here are two miracles: a pregnancy that involves no corruption and a birth that is virginal.

The angel said to her: *Hail, full of grace, the Lord is with you.* He is with you in your heart, with you in your belly, with you in your womb, with you in help given. Rejoice, blessed Virgin, for Christ the king has come from heaven into your womb; therefore shall you be blessed among women, for you have given birth to life for men and women alike.

The mother of our race brought punishment upon the world; the mother of our Lord brought salvation to it. Eve struck down, Mary gave life, as disobedience was replaced by obedience. In joy therefore does Mary bring forth her child, in gladness she embraces her son, she carries him by whom she is carried. Listen to what she says: *My soul magnifies the Lord, and my spirit rejoices in God my savior; for he has looked upon the lowliness of his handmaid; from this time forth all generations will call me blessed, because he who is mighty has done great things for me.*

After this prophecy of blessing, and while the Virgin is silently asking herself what the greeting may mean, the heavenly messenger continues: *Do not be afraid, Mary, for you have found favor with God; you will conceive and bear a son, and you shall name him Jesus.* But she answers: *How can this be since I do not know any man?* The angel responds: *The Holy Spirit will come upon you, and the power of the Most High will overshadow you; therefore the holy one to be born of you will be called the Son of God.*

Let us likewise rejoice on the day of this great Virgin who alone among women merited to conceive in her holy and chaste body, her virginal womb, the king whom the heavens, earth, and sea cannot contain. May she lovingly intercede for us with her Son who transported her so gloriously to the palace of heaven and who now lives and reigns for endless ages. Amen.

Homily 28 on Mary

Saint Paschasius Radbert (790-865), *a Benedictine monk and abbot, dedicated his life to writing, through which he helped to establish the doctrine on the eucharist. In one of his letters he writes about the Virgin's assumption and aludes to her immaculate conception.*

Today the glorious, ever-virgin Mary ascends to heaven. I urge you to rejoice, for, if I may so put it, she has been raised up in an ineffable way to be with Christ who reigns for ever. The Queen of the world is today taken from the earth and from this present evil time. I say again: rejoice, because she who is sure of her imperishable glory has reached the palace of heaven.

Exult, I say, and rejoice, and let the whole world rejoice because this day salvation has drawn nearer for us all.

Hail, Mary, full of grace; the Lord is with you; blessed are you among women. It was fitting that the Virgin should be given such gifts and be full of grace, since she has bestowed glory on heaven and has brought God and peace to the earth, faith to pagans, an end to vice, order to life, and discipline to morals.

And it was right that an angel be sent to the Virgin, because virginity always means kinship with the angels. *Rejoice,* the angel says, *for you are full of grace.* Yes, full! for while a share of grace was given to others, the undiminished fullness of grace was poured into Mary.

Letter

Toward the Dogma of the Immaculate Conception
First Phase

1054 — This was the year of the Great Schism between East and West. The role of Mary in writings takes on a different aspect. The origins of Mary play an important part. A feast of her conception, established in England (1060), gradually takes root in Europe.

Mary's Immaculate Conception will dominate theological thought on Mary for centuries. Perhaps the dogma of the Immaculate Conception would have been defined earlier if it were not for the political upheavals of the times.

In the middle of the twelfth century the feast of Mary's conception was introduced into Lyons in France; it had been introduced into England beforehand. Five centuries earlier the same feast under the title of the "conception of Saint Anne" was already popular in the Church of the East. Nor did the feast ever meet with any opposition on the part of the faithful in France or elsewhere.

It is an irony of history that the first to challenge directly the doctrinal import of the feast of our Lady's conception is Saint Bernard who is one of the most prolific writers on marian doctrine. Others too disagreed with this doctrine, but most, if not all, were prepared to relinquish their views if the Church should ever decide otherwise.

Saint Peter Damian (d.1072), *monk, bishop, and cardinal, worked for reform in the Church and religious life. He reflects on Mary's birth: First a house had to be built in which the king of heaven might deign to be a guest.*

The birth of the blessed and undefiled Mother of God justly brings human beings a special and indeed unparalleled joy, for it marked the beginning of all human salvation.

Almighty God in his ineffable providence knew, even before human beings were created, that they would perish because of the devil's intrigues, but, again before the ages began, his infinite love also formed a plan for their redemption. Not only did he establish, as part of this infinitely wise plan, the manner and order of redemption; he also determined beforehand the moment in time when he would carry out his plan.

Just as the human race could not be redeemed unless the Son of God were born of the Virgin, so too the Virgin had to be born from whom the Word was to become flesh. That is, first a house had to be built in which the king of heaven might deign to descend and be a guest. I refer to the house of which God said through Solomon: *Wisdom built itself a house and hewed seven columns for it.* This virginal house rested on seven columns, because the venerable mother of God was endowed with the seven gifts of the Holy Spirit. The bridal chamber had first to be constructed that would receive the bridegroom as he came for his marriage with holy Church.

Homily 45 on Mary

Michel Psellos (1018-1079), *statesman and philosopher, wrote on a variety of subjects. He uses Eastern imagery like deification (becoming like gods) to explain the meaning of Christ's coming. Mary's reply to the angel helped humanity to become one with the Godhead.*

Because human nature was destined to be totally deified, the beginning of this completely supernatural work had to be in harmony with the whole. Christ therefore became man to deify humanity by his union with it.

If the end is amazing, how much more so the means! If the ascent defies all description, how much more does the descent surpass all understanding! On the one hand, our mortal nature went up to heaven; on the other, God came down from heaven. The Incomprehensible became comprehensible; the Creator of human nature united himself with that nature; he who is impalpable and immaterial was born of a virgin! What words are adequate when we come to ponder this mystery?

Oh the marvel of it! We sinned and were punished, but now we are deemed worthy of still greater blessings! We lost paradise and have gained a dwelling place in heaven! We fell down to earth and have received our promised abode on high! And what is still more amazing is that the good news of this joy did not precede it, as is usual among humankind, but at the same time as the angel made his announcement to the Virgin, God who was announced became flesh, and the body he assumed was deified, the estranged were united, the oppressed set free, exiles were welcomed home, enemies reconciled! One brief word of greeting was addressed to the Mother of God, and instantly occurred consequences which can neither be counted nor comprehended.

Homily on Mary

Saint Anselm (1033-1109), *a Benedictine monk and archbishop of Canterbury, made an outstanding contribution to the thought of his day. He relied heavily on the writings of Augustine and was an ardent follower of the Augustinian school. His writings, especially his homilies, resound with Augustinian themes.*

How can I speak worthily of her who begot my Lord? Through her fruitfulness I have been delivered from my captivity, because she bore a child I have been redeemed from eternal death. Through her son I have been rescued from my ruin and brought back from misfortune to the blessed country. *Blessed are you among women, and blessed is the fruit of your womb* which has given me all this through the regeneration of baptism. It has given it to me in reality or in hope, even though I myself may be deprived of everything and on the verge of despair. Well, then, if my sins are forgiven, shall I be so ungrateful to her through whom so many blessings have come, quite freely, to me? May God preserve me from adding this injustice to my iniquities.

God gave his Son, the fruit of his heart, who was his equal and whom he loved like himself. He gave him to Mary, and of Mary's womb he made his Son not someone else but his Son, in person, so that he is by his nature the only Son of God and of Mary. The whole creation is the work of God, and God is born of Mary! God created everything and Mary gave birth to God! God who forms everything was himself formed in Mary's womb, and so he made again all that he had made.

He who was able to make all things out of nothing was not willing to remake his destroyed creation until he had first become the son of Mary. God is thus the Father of all created things, and Mary is the mother of all that has been re-created. God is the Father of the worldwide creation, and Mary is the mother of the worldwide redemption. For God begot him through whom all things were made, and Mary gave birth to him through whom everything has been saved.

O Mother, blessed and exalted not for yourself alone but also for us, what do I perceive coming to us through you? How great it is and how worthy of love! What I see rejoices me with a joy that I dare not express. If, our Lady, you are his mother, are not your other sons his brothers? But what brothers and of whom? Shall I say what I ardently believe, or should I keep silence, lest I should seem vainglorious? But what I ardently believe, why should I not utter its praise? I shall speak, then, not out of vanity, but out of gratitude. For he who was willing, in being born of a mother, to share our nature, and, in restoring life to us, to make us the sons of his mother, it is even he who invites us to acknowledge ourselves to be his brothers. Our judge is thus our Brother. The Savior of the world is our Brother. In a word, our God made himself, through Mary, our Brother.

Homily 7 on Mary

*This **Augustinian text** of the twelfth century shows how Mary's origins and her end are uppermost in the minds of writers. In this text we obtain a glimpse of concern over the assumption of Mary into heaven, a truth which became dogma later on.*

The totality of the world shows forth the extent of Christ's power; Mary's integrity shows forth the extent of her grace. What so strange, then, if in this great variety of privileges, we say that she suffered death, the common lot of all humanity, and yet that she was not bound down by death's chains, she through whom God willed to be born and to share the substance of flesh? Surely this will not be impious. For we know that Jesus can do all things.

The throne of God, the bridal chamber of the Lord of heaven, the dwelling and tabernacle of Christ is worthy to be there where he himself is. That the most sacred body, then, from which Christ assumed flesh was handed over to be the food of worms, I cannot bring myself to believe.

I hold that we must confess with good reason that Mary is in Christ and with Christ: in Christ, because in him we live and move and have our being; with Christ gloriously assumed to the joys of eternity.

If anyone should choose to gainsay the assumption, since he would not deny that Christ could bring it about, let him advance reasons to show that it would not become Christ to will to do it, and therefore that it was not done. And if he shall show that he truly knows the mind of God in the matter, I will begin to accept from him what otherwise I have not dared to imagine.

PL 40, 1140-1148

Ivo of Chartres (1040-1115) *belonged to the Canons Regular of Saint Augustine and later became bishop of Chartres. He wrote extensively and was a remarkable theologian. In this passage from one of the twenty-five homilies preserved, he manifests his totally spiritual conception of the Church as he reflects on Mary as the instrument of God in bringing Christ to us.*

If the Lord of all was going to come in search of his runaway slaves to sit in judgment rather than show compassion, he would never have put on our frail mortal clay in order to suffer with us and for us. To use Paul's words, this might seem foolish and weak to the Gentiles who, relying on the specious arguments of philosophy, judge the Creator by the laws that govern creation. But what could be more striking evidence of his power than to give the Virgin a son against the laws of nature, and through his death in the human nature he had assumed to summon mortal humanity to immortal glory? As the Apostle wrote: *God's weakness is stronger than human strength.*

There is a profound and wonderful mystery in the conception by which the bond of our transgression is cancelled. The divine is joined to the human, and two, that is Christ and the Church, become one body. The Virgin's womb was the bridal chamber for this union, and at the end of the normal period for carrying a child, Christ together with his spouse, our flesh, *like a bridegroom leaving his chamber, placed his dwelling,* the body he had assumed, *in the sun;* for he made his body through which he was to vanquish the foe visible to all.

Homily 15 on the Annunciation

Eadmer of Canterbury (1060-1124), *a Benedictine and follower of Saint Anselm, was a hagiographer and devotional writer. He wrote a treatise on Mary's conception which contains the first theological defense of the doctrine of the Immaculate Conception and foreshadows in a remarkable way some of the later arguments on this theme. In this passage by Eadmer of Canterbury we see Mary's role extolled, and this will continue to happen more and more in subsequent authors.*

Any supreme honor that God ever willed for another than himself he undoubtedly willed for you, O blessed among women. For he willed to make you his Mother, and because he willed it, he did it. What am I saying! He, the Creator, the sovereign Master of all things, made you his Mother! He, the Author and Lord of all beings, not only those that are intelligible but those that transcend every intellect, made you, our Lady, his only Mother and Empress of the universe! You thus became the Sovereign and Queen of the heavens, lands, and seas, of all the elements and everything they contain.

It was for this destiny that he formed you by the action of the Holy Spirit, in the womb of your mother, from the very first instant of your conception. So it is, good Lady, and we rejoice that it is so. But, sweet Mary, for whom such greatness was stored up and who was destined to become sole Mother of the Supreme Good and, after your Son, prudent and noble Ruler of all beings past, present, and future: could you have been in your origin one who ought to be put on the level, or even beneath, of any of the creatures over whom, we are sure, you now exercise dominion?

Tract on the Conception of Mary

Saint Bernard (1090-1153), *whose mystical works had great influence in forming the mysticism of the middle ages, became famous for his life as a reformer and for his service to the Church. In these passages he shows how he is a doctor of marian thought. He calls us Mary's slaves who confidently follow our mistress.*

The glorious Virgin has ascended into heaven, surely filling up the measure of joy of those who dwell there. If the soul of an unborn child melted in bliss when Mary spoke, what was the joy of the heavenly citizens when they not only heard her voice but saw her face and enjoyed her blessed presence among them? The whole universe is lit up by the presence of Mary, so much so that even heaven itself, irradiated with the light of her virginal brightness, takes on a new resplendence. Rightly then do praise and thanksgiving resound on high, but it might seem more fitting for us to cry rather than clap our hands! If heaven rejoices in Mary's presence, does it not follow that our world below should proportionately bemoan her absence?

But let that be the end of our repining, for here we have no abiding city: we seek the very city to which blessed Mary has gone. If we are enrolled as citizens of heaven, it is surely right for us to remember her and to share her happiness even in our exile, even here beside the waters of Babylon. Our queen has gone before us, and so glorious has been her entry into paradise that we, her slaves, confidently follow our mistress, crying: *Draw us after you and we shall run in the fragance of your perfumes.* As mother of our judge and mother of mercy, she will humbly and efficaciously handle the affairs of our salvation.

Earth has sent a priceless gift up to heaven, so that by giving and receiving within the blessed bond of friendship, the human is wedded to the divine, earth to heaven, the depths to the heights. A sublime fruit of the earth has gone up to heaven, from which alone descend the best gifts, the perfect gifts. The Blessed Virgin has ascended on high, and therefore she too will give gifts to human beings. And why not? Surely neither the ability nor the will to do so is lacking to her. She is the queen of heaven; she is compassionate; finally, she is the mother of the only begotten Son of God. And nothing can so commend the greatness of her power or her love unless perhaps we do not believe that the Son of God honors his mother, or unless we doubt Mary's maternity (which means that Love itself that is born of God rested within her physically for nine months) evoked a response of love in her heart. But this I say for our benefit, knowing that perfect charity which seeks not its own is not easily found in the midst of our great misery.

In the meantime (passing over in silence the benefits that will accrue to us through her glorification) if we love her, we shall indeed rejoice because she has gone to her Son. We shall congratulate her without reserve, unless — which God forbid — we shall be found wholly without gratitude toward her who has re-found for us the way of grace. The Lord, whom she first received when he entered the village of this world, receives her into the holy city.   *Homily 7 on Mary*

Blessed Guerric of Igny (1070/80-1157) *was a Cistercian monk whose spirituality was influenced by Origen. His sermons to his monks have been preserved; in them he spoke often on Mary. In this passage the motherhood of Mary is emphasized in contrast to the motherhood of Eve. Mary, like the Church of which she is a model, is the mother of all who are born again to new life.*

One and unique was Mary's child, the only Son of his Father in heaven and the only Son of his mother on earth. Mary alone was virgin-mother, and it is her glory to have borne the Father's only Son. But now she embraces that only Son of hers in all his members. She is not ashamed to be called the mother of all those in whom she recognizes that Christ her Son has been or is on the point of being formed.

Our ancient mother Eve was more of a stepmother than a true mother, passing on to her children the sentence of death before bringing them into the light of day. Her name indeed means "mother of all the living," but she proved more truly to be the slayer of the living or the mother of the dying, since for her to give birth was to transmit death.

Eve being unable to respond faithfully to the meaning of her name, its mysterious import was fully expressed by Mary. Like the Church of which she is the model, Mary is the mother of all who are born again to new life. She is the mother of him who is the Life by which all things live; when she bore him, she gave new birth in a sense to all who were to live by his life.

Recognizing that by virtue of this mystery she is the mother of all Christians, Christ's blessed mother also shows herself a mother to them by her care and loving kindness. She never grows hard toward her children, as though they were not her own. The womb that once gave birth is not dried up; it continues to bring forth the fruit of her tender compassion. Christ, the blessed fruit of that womb, left his mother still fraught with inexhaustible love, a love that once came forth from her but remains always within her, inundating her with his gifts.

It can be seen that the children themselves recognize her as their mother. A natural instinct, inspired by faith, prompts them to have recourse to her in all dangers and difficulties, invoking her and taking refuge in her arms like little ones running to their mother. To this day we dwell in the shelter of the mother of the Most High, remaining under her protection as it were beneath the shadow of her wings. And in the days to come we shall share in her glory; we shall know the warmth of her loving embrace. Then there will be one joyful voice proclaiming the praise of our mother: Holy Mother of God, *in you we all find our home!*

Homily 1 on Mary's Assumption 2-4

Saint Amadeus of Lausanne (1110-1159), Cistercian abbot of Hautcombe and later bishop of Lausanne, was encouraged by his abbot, Saint Bernard of Clairvaux, to positions of leadership. He was the author of eight marian homilies, the seventh of which was cited twice in the 1950 papal definition of the dogma of the Assumption. In this homily he casts Mary as one who intercedes at the throne of her son. The tone reminds us of the prayer Salve, Regina (Hail, Holy Queen), which dates back to the eleventh century.

The glorious Virgin was, with flesh untouched and tranquil mind, the gentlest of the living: the more lowly and more holy she is than all others, the higher was she raised above all until she was received into heaven by its citizens with every mark of honor. There in the fashion of a queen, she was bidden by the supreme Father to sit down in the kingdom of eternal brightness and on the throne of surpassing glory, first in rank after the Son whom she born incarnate.

Mighty God, terrible and strong, of unspeakable goodness, you raise and exalt your humble handmaid to the place from which you had long ago driven out your jealous foe, so that humility might triumph, adorned by you with the increase of grace and a glorious crown, while pride, empty and dark, might fall in ruin.

Conspicuous therefore by her unparalleled merit the blessed Lady stands before the face of her Creator interceding always for us with her powerful prayer. Taught by that light to which all things are bare and open, she sees our dangers, and, our merciful and sweet lady, pities us with motherly affection. The more she beholds from on high the heart of the mighty king the more profoundly she knows, by the grace of divine pity, how to pity the unhappy and to help the afflicted.

Homily 8 in Praise of the Blessed Virgin Mary

Solomon says that there is a time for joy and a time for grief. Grief has departed, the time for joy has come, that true joy which proceeds from Christ's resurrection. For he has risen and he has raised up his mother's soul. She lay as in a narrow tomb of grief while the Lord lay on the sepulcher. As he arose, her spirit lived again and, waking as if from deep slumber, she saw in the morning light the sun of justice and the rays of his rising. She gazed upon the beginning of the rising dawn and the future resurrection of her flesh, coming before time in her son. She feasted her eyes upon the glowing flesh of the risen Lord and in her heart perceived the glory of his godhead, so that within and without, leaving and entering, she enjoyed the pastorage of true and everlasting felicity. Beside herself, therefore forgetting self for joy, she clung with all her heart to the Father of spirits and bound fast to God she poured out upon him her whole self and was wholly flooded in the immensity of his love.

Lord, in your strength she rejoiced greatly and she will exult mightily in your saving help. You have granted her her heart's desire and not withheld from her the request of her life, since you have anticipated her with sweet blessings. You have placed on her head a crown of precious stones.

Homily 6 in Praise of the Blessed Virgin Mary

***Saint Aelred of Rievaulx** (1109-1167), a Cistercian monk and also abbot, combines mystical and speculative theology in his writings. Many concepts and phrases in these writings are similar to those of Saint Augustine. In this passage Aelred speaks of Mary's sublime exaltation.*

If Saul, still breathing threats and murder against the disciples of the Lord to the extent of persecuting the Lord himself, became the object of such great mercy that as a result he himself was able to glory in the hope of the glory of the children of God, if he was — whether in his body or out of his body — caught up to the third heaven, there is no reason to be surprised that the holy Mother of God, who had lived with her Son through all his trials from his earliest infancy, was raised bodily to heaven and exalted above the choirs of angels.

If there is joy among the angels when a single sinner repents, how can one describe the joyful, wonderful praise that goes up to God for the Virgin Mary who never sinned nor spoke a single false word? If it is true that those who were formerly darkness can become light in the Lord, shining like the sun in the kingdom of their Father, who can describe the eternal weight of the glory of the Virgin Mary, the glory of her who appeared in this world like the glowing dawn, fair as the moon, clear as the sun, of her from whom came forth the true light, enlightening every person coming into the world?

Since the Lord said, *If any one serves me, he must follow me, and where I am, there shall my servant be also,* where, do you think, will his mother be, she who served him with such faithful constancy?

Homily on the Assumption of Mary

*The ecclesiology of **Blessed Isaac of Stella** (1105/20-1178), a Cistercian monk of English origin who became abbot of Stella, has its roots in the theology of Saint Augustine. He sees the mystery of Christ as dynamic and ever present today, for the mysteries of Christ are continued in the mystery of the Church. The divine motherhood of Mary may be compared with the motherhood of the Church.*

The Son of God is the firstborn of many brothers and sisters. Although by nature he is God's only Son, by grace he has joined many to himself and made them one with him, for *he has given* those who receive him *power to become children of God.*

He became the Son of man and made many men and women children of God, uniting them to himself by his love and power so that they became as one. In themselves they are many by reason of their human descent, but in him they are one by divine rebirth.

The whole and unique Christ — the head and the body — is one, born of one God in heaven and one mother on earth. This Christ is both many sons and one son. And as head and members are one son and many, so Mary and the Church are one mother and many mothers, one virgin and many virgins. Both are mothers, both are virgins. Each conceives of the same Spirit without concupiscence. Each is Christ's mother, but neither gives birth to the whole Christ without the cooperation of the other.

In the inspired scriptures what is said in general of
the virgin mother the Church is understood in
particular of the Virgin Mary, and what is said in
particular of the virgin mother Mary is rightly understood in a general sense of the virgin mother the
Church. What is said of either can be understood of
both almost without qualification. Every believing
soul is also, in its own way, a virginal and fruitful bride
of the Word of God and a mother, daughter, and
sister of Christ.

That this is so of the Church in general, of Mary in
particular and of every believer individually, the very
Wisdom of God, the Father's Word, declares in the
text: *I will dwell in the inheritance of the Lord.* The
Lord's inheritance is the Church in its totality, Mary in
a very special sense and also each individual believer.
Christ dwelt for nine months in the tabernacle of
Mary's womb. He dwells until the end of the ages in
the tabernacle of the Church's faith. He will dwell for
ever in the knowledge and love of each faithful soul.

Sermon 51

Saint Thomas Aquinas (1225-1274) of the Dominican Order, heavily influenced by Saint Augustine, has guided the teaching of theology for centuries. In his monumental work Summa Theologica *he speaks about Mary's role in salvation history and in the realm of grace. Like Saint Bernard, Saint Thomas Aquinas says that the whole world benefited from Mary's reply to the incarnation.*

It is related that the angel said to Mary: *Behold, you shall conceive in your womb and shall bring forth a son.* It was reasonable that it should be announced to the Blessed Virgin that she was to conceive Christ. First, in order to maintain a becoming order in the union of Son of God with the Virgin — namely, that she should be informed in mind concerning him, before conceiving him in the flesh. Thus Augustine says: "Mary is more blessed in receiving the faith of Christ than in conceiving the flesh of Christ." And further on he adds: "Her nearness as a mother would have been of no profit to Mary, had she not borne Christ in her heart after a more blessed manner than in her flesh."

Secondly, that she might be a more certain witness of this mystery, being instructed therein by God. Thirdly, that she might offer to God the free gift of her obedience: which she proved herself right ready to do, saying: *Behold the handmaid of the Lord.* Fourthly, in order to show that there is a certain spiritual wedlock between the Son of God and human nature. Wherefore in the Annunciation the Virgin's consent was besought in lieu of that of the entire human nature.

Summa Theologica, q. 30, art. 1

In the same century another professor in Paris, **Saint Bonaventure** *(1217-1274) of the Franciscan Order and later cardinal bishop of Albano, Italy, played an important part in the events of the Council of Lyons (1274). He wrote of the Annunciation and of Mary's role in the economy of grace.*

When the angel announced to the Blessed Virgin Mary the mystery of the incarnation to be accomplished within her, she believed it, desired it, and consented to it. Whereupon she was sanctified and made fruitful by the overshadowing of the Holy Spirit. Through his power, "virginal was her conceiving of the Son of God, virginal her birth-giving, and virginal her state after deliverance," as Saint Augustine says. She conceived not only a body, but a body with a soul, a body united to the Word and free from the stain of sin, a body all-holy and immaculate. That is why she is called the Mother of God, and is yet also the most sweet Virgin Mary.

As it was a woman deceived by Satan and carnally known and corrupted by her husband's lust who handed down sin, sickness, and death to all, so it was a woman instructed by an angel and made holy and fruitful by the Holy Spirit who gave birth without taint of soul or body to an offspring, the giver of grace, health, and life to all who come to him.

Thus, the Blessed Virgin became a mother in the most complete sense, for, without man, she conceived the Son of God through the action of the Holy Spirit. Because the love of the Holy Spirit burned so intensely in her soul, the power of the Holy Spirit wrought marvels in her flesh, by means of grace prompting, assisting, elevating her nature as required for this wondrous conception. *Breviloquium IV, 3, 1.2.5*

Scholastics and Mystics

In the fourteenth and fifteenth centuries scholastics and mystics write about Mary under her title of the Immaculate Conception. In a sense we have the remote preparation for the dogma of the Immaculate Conception, even though writers of previous centuries have also alluded to it. The writers of these centuries prepare for the future, namely, what was said at the Council of Basel in 1439 and in the dogma proclaimed in the nineteenth century by Pope Pius IX.

Blessed Giles of Rome (1243-1316), a pupil and ardent follower of Saint Thomas Aquinas, soared past his master and began what is known today as the Augustinian school of theology. He wrote masterful treatises on philosophy, theology, and politics; he also composed some prayers, for example, the Soul of Christ (Anima Christi), echoes of which can be seen in this passage. His sermons have never been found, but the following passage on Mary's role as mother shows how his theological and speculative mind flows into his spirituality.

Christ's conception was miraculous insofar as no human father or human seed had part in it. But his conception was not miraculous as far as his mother was concerned, for she simply supplied the material, namely, blood, from which the power of the Holy Spirit formed the body of Christ.

Furthermore, it was his birth from the Virgin that gave Christ the same nature as her; it was as a human being born of another human being that he belonged to the same species as his virginal Mother.

A further point: Christ indeed came forth in a miraculous manner from the Virgin's womb, but it does not follow from this that he was not her natural son. She supplied the material for his human body and thus played the role in the conception and birth of her child that any true mother plays in the natural course of things. In the very instant in which she said, *Behold the handmaid of the Lord,* she enclosed in her womb a human being. The Word was in her womb; the Word became flesh, that is, a human being.

Commentary on the Sentences, pars III

Meister John Eckhart (1260-1327), *a Dominican and a teacher at Paris, wrote much on theology and at times was misunderstood. Meister Eckhart, continuing the tradition of one of his contemporaries, the elder Henry of Friemar, O.S.A., says that what happened to Mary happens to each one of us. Also, continuing the tradition of Saint Bernard, Meister, as he was referred to, says that the Holy Spirit did not speak the word only to her, but that he spoke it to a great multitude, to every good soul that longs for God.*

If Mary had not first given spiritual birth to God, he would never have been born bodily from her. A woman said to our Lord: *Blessed is the womb that bore you.* Then our Lord said: *It is not only the womb which bore me that is blessed; they are blessed who hear God's word and keep it.* It is more precious to God to be born spiritually from every such virgin or from every good soul than that he was bodily born of Mary.

In this we must understand that we must be an only son whom the Father has eternally begotten. When the Father begot all created things, then he begot me, and I flowed out with all created things, and yet I remained within, in the Father. In the same way, when the word that I am now speaking springs up in me, there is a second process as I rest upon the image, and a third when I pronounce it and you all receive it; and yet properly it remains within me. So I have remained within the Father. In the Father are the images of all created things. This piece of wood has a rational image in God. It is not merely rational, but it is pure reason.

The greatest good that God ever performed for humanity was that he became man. I ought to tell a story now that is very apposite here. There were a rich husband and wife. Then the wife suffered a misfortune through which she lost an eye, and she was much distressed by this. Then her husband came to her and said: "Madam, why are you so distressed? You should not distress yourself so, because you have lost your eye." Then she said: "Sir, I am not distressing myself about the fact that I have lost my eye; what distresses me is that it seems to me that you will love me less because of it." Then he said: "Madam, I do love you."

Not long after that he gouged out one of his own eyes and came to his wife and said: "Madam, to make you believe that I love you, I have made myself like you; now I too have only one eye." This stands for man and woman, who could scarcely believe that God loved them so much, until God gouged out one of his own eyes and took upon himself human nature. This is what *being made flesh* is. Our Lady said: *How should this happen?* Then the angel said: *The Holy Spirit will come down from above into you,* from the highest throne, from the Father of eternal light.

Sermon 22: Ave, gratia plena

Henry of Friemar the Elder (or Henry of Germany) (d.1340), an Augustinian, was influenced by Giles of Rome. He passed on to the Augustinian Order valuable historical data, but he likewise wrote treatises on the spiritual life, especially on discernment. In these passages Henry highlights the holiness of Mary.

Mary clearly showed us her possession of the full attainment of interior purity and the beauty that virtue gives when, according to Bernard, she was robed in the sun of divine brightness. For this reason she is rightly regarded as symbolized in the great sign which John saw in heaven when he saw a woman clothed with the sun. For according to Bernard, to the extent that the unsullied natural condition allows she is immersed in inaccessible light to a greater extent than are all other created spirits.

It is clear that the refulgent overshadowing of the devout mind by the light in which it can contemplate God was brilliantly present in Mary; for, according to Bernard, the Holy Spirit so overshadowed her with the light of divine wisdom that she had perfect knowledge of all the divine plans which God in his mercy had decided to carry out in her regard. All this is evident from the fact that she herself made known these hidden mysteries in intimate conversation with the writers who set down the truth of the gospel.

The shining transfiguration of the face of Christ signifies that by the power of the divine light the image in the rational soul is divinized through transformation into its uncreated model, as the Apostle teaches: *But we, beholding with unveiled face the glory of the Lord, are transformed from glory to glory, into an image of the same, as by the Spirit of the Lord.* This aspect likewise shines forth for us in Mary, because her mind was so wholly conformed by grace to its eternal model that she can be called, without parallel, the seal of the divine likeness and the exalted resting place of the entire Trinity. This transformation brings the final perfection to the bridal bed of the soul and to the spiritual beauty of the knowing mind, which is intended to conceive the eternal Word mentally by grace. In this conception the devout mind is flooded with the ineffable sweetness of which Augustine speaks so beautifully in the third book of his work *Free Will:* "So great is the beauty of the eternal light that if we could dwell in it for even a single moment, we would rightly regard as naught a thousand years of delights." May a share in this beauty be granted us by him who is blessed through all ages. Amen.

Treatise on the Coming of the Word in the Mind 1, 4

Blessed Simon Fidati of Cascia (1285-1348), one of the greatest preachers in Italy during his era, was an Augustinian friar. His writings are steeped in scripture and rich in feeling. In these selections he speaks of Mary as handmaiden and child of the Lord.

Imagine how reverently the angel stood before this glorious village girl, knowing that she was to be the mother of the Son of God! See and contemplate how humbly and modestly she listened and gave answer to the angel who had come as ambassador and was awaiting her reply.

What would you have done if you had been at the door of this room or cell and had heard this holy, pleasing dialogue between this blessed girl and the angel? Would not your heart have been sweetly riven by great joy and boundless consolation? Harder than stone and steel is the heart that is not riven as it reads or hears or thinks about the words the virgin spoke to the angel and the angel to the virgin. Would you not have cried aloud, humbly but very fervently and from a full heart: "Sweet Madonna, kindest of women, I beg you, agree quickly to what the angel says, so that your Son may deliver us from the damnation in which our first mother has put us!"

What would you have said and done, Christian soul, when you heard the Virgin Mary say to the angel: *I am the servant and handmaiden of the Lord; be it done to me according to your word?* At that moment, the power of the Holy Spirit immediately formed and generated the body of Christ from the pure blood of the Virgin, infused the newly created soul into that body, and united the divinity inseparably with that soul and body. *The Gospels, I, 2*

In addition to much else, we have in the gospel of the visitation three very powerful lessons or examples from our Lady, the Virgin Mary.

The first example is of charity that cannot be idle but is always active, so ordering soul and body that now the one, now the other is doing some good work. Mary, filled with love, first received God's consolation and lesson through the angel, and devoted her soul to praise and contemplation and to devout prayer. Then, when the angel had departed, she immediately set out and went to devote herself to corporal works of mercy and charity by serving Elizabeth, who was pregnant and had the work of the house. So ought every Christian soul to act. After receiving some lesson from God and exercising the soul in one or other manner, by reading or hearing the word of God or by contemplating and reflecting on God and his will or by praising and praying in accordance with the grace received, the soul should set aside these spiritual actions and turn immediately to bodily actions, exercising the body in some good work that serves God or the neighbor for love of God or for the needs of one's own body.

The second lesson and example is of profound humility. Solomon says: *The greater you are, the more you should humble yourself, and you will find favor with God and human beings.* Therefore the Virgin Mary, though her mind was filled with the words of God and though she had been chosen and made Mother of God and Queen of paradise, was not reluctant to go and serve Elizabeth as a maid and be with her and the other women, not as a mistress but as a servant. She was not ashamed to serve, but took delight in it. So ought every Christian man and woman act. They ought not to be disdainful or reluctant but should readily and joyfully go and serve persons of lesser degree than themselves, so that by imitating and becoming like Christ and his Mother in this life, they may deserve to become their companions in the next. For we must be certain that the man or woman who is not their companion in the actions and habits of this life will not be their companion in the other life.

From Elizabeth, too, we can derive a lesson and example of humility. For when the Mother of God visited her, she did not show herself ungrateful and proud, as many people do whom others serve. Rather she was grateful and humble, praising and thanking the Virgin Mary: *Whence this great favor, that the Mother of my Lord God should come to serve me?* She did not consider herself worthy of this service.

The third lesson and example is of great wisdom. When the Virgin Mary was thanked and praised by Elizabeth, she did not foolishly grow vain but, being wise and humble, was abashed instead and made little of herself by praising and thanking God from whom every grace and virtue comes. She did the same while she stayed with Elizabeth for three months and then returned to her own home.

Lofty and profound conversations on wonderful things did these great prophetesses have when they first met. Nor did they quickly part again, for each found the company of the other very pleasant and charming. They were filled with heavenly blessings and favors, pregnant with wonderful sons, and vehicles of the works of the Holy Spirit. Therefore they yearned, in affections and words, for spiritual things, even if not equally, since the one was superior to the other in every respect. They also judged it good and very sweet to keep company and to remain together for a while so that they might speak to one another of God and virtue (for they did not know how to speak of things earthly and sinful).

What spiritual joy and gladness we must believe these two blessed souls experienced as they spoke exclusively of things divine, each telling the other that it was not because of their own merits and goodness but solely by divine grace that they had become mothers of two such great and noble sons!

These two women whom heavenly love had united could not bear to part from one another. Elizabeth, though elderly, did not banish Mary, a young girl, or send her home, but rather gently asked and persuaded her to remain, for she was convinced that as long as she continued to have in her house the Son of God, who was present there in his virginal Mother, she would be enriched and exalted; and this she greatly desired. Nor did the young virgin want to be separated from the elderly housewife, for she had come in haste to see her with the desire of remaining until the birth of John, of whose conception she knew from the angelic revelation and whom she realized was to be her Son's precursor and the preacher who would prepare the way for him.

Reflect, then, Christian soul, on these holy lessons and examples and know that we should not easily and without solid reason abandon the company of good persons, when it is possible to remain with them.

We should not lightly leave the company of those whom we truly believe and know to be possessed of virtue. In fact, it is a tested sign of virtuous people that they willingly remain with the good and find it wearisome to depart from them. To remain perseveringly with the virtuous is true life and a practice that brings no harm. When active lovers of the heavenly virtues gather to give and receive example from one another, they are constrained to live in such a way that they advance from good to better.

The Gospels, I, 3

Hermann of Schildesche (d.1357), *an Augustinian scholar and mystic, dedicates an entire work to the conception of the Blessed Virgin. At this period there was much speculation on the immaculate conception of Mary, which had not yet been declared a dogma of faith. Having expressed his opinion, Hermann of Schildesche concludes his treatise with these moving words.*

From all this I conclude that, whatever opinion be held regarding the conception of the Blessed Virgin, there is nothing in it to make the celebration of this holy feast deserving of anything less than complete respect.

And because I, though an unworthy and useless panegyrist, have with the Lord's help written these things to praise the glorious Virgin, I think it right to end this treatise with praise of her. I shall therefore conclude this little work by citing the words with which the glorious doctor Augustine ends his sermon on the assumption: "O Blessed Virgin Mary, who can worthily give you due thanks and praise for coming to the aid of a hopeless world with your unparalleled consent? What tribute can be paid you by a weak human race that has access to healing solely through the exchange that took place in you? Nonetheless, gracious Virgin, receive courteously my poor thanks that fall so short of your merits. And when you have received my offering, win forgiveness for my sins by praying for me to your Son, our Lord and judge." And, further on: "You are the sole hope of sinners. They hope to win through you forgiveness of their offenses; and in you, most blessed one, is our expectation of reward."

Finally, since there are no real proofs in the area I have been discussing, all may legitimately maintain what they think more suitable and consistent with praise of God and the merits of the Blessed Virgin. Let my readers not be satisfied to disparage what I have said in this little work; let them rather seek to discuss it devoutly, correct what needs correction, and turn everything to the praise of Christ and the glorious Virgin. If they have a better understanding than I of any point, let them thank Christ and the Blessed Virgin and, with loving compassion, turn my ignorance to their advancement in salvation.

I think I may humbly ask for such a reading especially from all true lovers of the Blessed Virgin Mary. It was out of devotion to her that I undertook this work of thought, word, and pen for the honor of Christ her Son, here in the esteemed diocese of Wurzburg. Let me conclude with the words which Blessed Augustine wrote to Dardanus in the thirty-ninth of his letters: I thus end this little work as though addressing any true lover of the Virgin: "If you think this work of my pen to be in any way useful, thank God; if you find defects of mine in it, forgive them as a dear friend would, granting me pardon and wishing me healing with one and same heartfelt love."

Tract on the Conception of the Virgin Mary, II, 10-12

Johann Tauler *(1300-1361) was a Dominican and a great preacher. He comprised the German mystical tradition of his time. During the darkest ages of the Black Death this fourteenth century mystic stayed behind in Strasburg to render practical and spiritual assistance to the sick and dying. As a disciple of Meister Eckhart he was influenced by the teachings of Augustine and the Augustinian school and thus portrays two important concepts of this school: our spiritual birth in Mary and the interiority of the Christian life.*

Until now we have spoken of the first and the last birth, and how the first should teach us about the last. But now we would like to also refer to the second birth, when God's Son was born on this night of the Mother and has become our brother. In eternity he was born without a mother, and in time he was born without a father. "Mary," so Saint Augustine tells us, "was more blessed because God was born spiritually in her soul than because he was born from her in the flesh." Now whoever wishes this birth to occur in his soul as nobly and as spiritually as it did in Mary's should reflect on the qualities which made her a mother both in spirit and in the flesh. She was a pure maiden, a virgin; she was betrothed, given in marriage; and she was turned inward, secluded from exterior things, when the angel came to her. And these are the qualities a spiritual mother ought to possess, should God be born in her soul.

The soul should be a pure and chaste virgin. And if it ever lost its purity, it should reverse its ways and become pure and virginal again. It should be a virgin, bringing forth no outward fruit (in the eyes of the world), but much fruit within. This also means shutting out external concerns, not paying too much attention to them, not expecting much reward from them. Mary's heart was fixed solely on the divine. *Sermon 1*

Writing from the Church of the East is **Nicholas Cabasilas**
*(1322-c.1389), a native of Thessalonica and a priest. In preaching on
Mary he emphasizes her role in the incarnation.*

When God was about to draw Eve from Adam's side,
far from telling him and persuading him, he deprived
him of his faculties and took away one of his members.
But in the case of Mary, he began by warning her and by
waiting for her act of faith before accomplishing his
work. Likewise, when he created Adam God spoke to
his Son alone, saying to him: *Let us make man.* But when
he was about to bring his firstborn into the world —
that wonderful Counselor — and to fashion the second
Adam, he included the Virgin in his planning. This great
counsel of which Isaiah speaks, this great plan, was announced by God and the Virgin ratified it.

The incarnation was not only the work of the Father
who decided on it, and the work of his power covering
the Virgin with his shadow, and the work of the Spirit
who came upon her; it was also the work of the Virgin's
will and faith. Without the Father, without his power
and his Spirit, such a project could not have taken
shape; without the will and faith of the Immaculate, the
divine counsel could not have been realized.

Behold, I am the handmaid of the Lord, she said. *Let it
be done to me according to your word.* She spoke, and the
result followed the word: *And the Word became flesh and
dwelt among us.* As soon as Mary had given God her
word, she received the Spirit which formed in her that
flesh wholly imbued with divinity.

Homily on the Annunciation 4-5.10

John Waldeby (1315-1372), *English Augustinian preacher and writer, shows that Mary is a preeminent person but still a member of the human race. Vatican II (Lumen gentium no. 53) also reiterated this message.*

The Lord is with you. This is the third part of the angel's greeting which specifically concerns the feast of the blessed Annunciation, when as soon as the Virgin had given her assent to it she received the Son of God in her womb. As Augustine says, "In speaking of her act of receiving: Give your word, and receive the Son."

By virtue of this it is to be noted that sin is nothing other than a withdrawal from God. In the words of the psalm: *Salvation is far from sinners.* As, in his *Confessions*, Augustine says that he found himself far from God in a different country. And as, in his Letter to Damasus on the prodigal son, Jerome explains the text in Luke 19: *He went away to a distant country.* Therefore the human race which sinned in Adam when he transgressed the divine command has been far from God for a very long time. But God *will not be angry for ever*, nor in his anger does he withhold his mercy. Though angry, he remembers to be merciful. And so he came to seek what had strayed off the right path into a wilderness, and also to save what had perished. But according to the Apostle: *It is not the angels he cares for, but the descendants of Abraham.* And he did not descend indiscriminately to any person, but to the blessed Virgin Mary who had been specially chosen for this — and with good reason.

You see that dew or rain descending from the sky reaches the mountains first, since they are nearest the sky, and descends down the mountains to the valleys. So the dew and rain of abundant mercy, in the person of Christ, came down to humanity in the incarnation, in which he reached Mary, the highest in sanctity, and remained in her, and from her took the body which in his mercy he gave for our salvation.

We read in the psalm: *The mountain in which God is pleased to dwell.* And elsewhere, *You have made the Most High your refuge.* Therefore just as a mountain in a certain manner is halfway between heaven and earth, so is the blessed Virgin. For it she bore a human body, yet she observed the kind of life that angels live, and so she was *a compact mountain, a rich mountain. A compact mountain,* compact of body and soul; *a rich mountain,* rich in divine grace, by which she is proclaimed complete, and this incarnation of Christ is made more certain through both evangelical and prophetic scripture. But it also seems consonant with both reason and natural order. For when learned people inquire into the form of the world, which is circular, and ask why God preferred to create the world in this form rather than any other, they answer it is in that form because that is the most perfect form, since nothing can be added to it, and it is also the most capacious form.

Ave Maria

Saint Catherine of Siena (1347-1380) is among the greatest teachers of spirituality. She learned everything from God. She emphasized in her teachings the Augustinian principles of self-knowledge, the Trinity, and the inner teacher, themes which she undoubtedly learned from her association with the Dominican Third Order and with the Augustinian friars of Lecceto, especially her spiritual friend, William Flete, O.S.A. In this passage she tells us of Jesus' reward in giving reverence to his mother.

Then that soul, in obedience to the high eternal Father, gazed into him with eager longing, and God eternal showed her the condemnation of the person in question. He said: I want you to know that I permitted this to happen to rescue him from the sentence of eternal damnation under which he stood, so that he might have life through his own blood of my Truth, my only-begotten Son. For I had not forgotten the reverence and love he had for Mary, my only-begotten Son's most gentle mother. For my goodness, in deference to the Word, has decreed that anyone at all, just or sinner, who holds her in due reverence will never be snatched or devoured by the infernal demon. She is like a bait set out by my goodness to catch my creatures. So it was in mercy that I did this. That is, though I did not make the evil intent of the wicked, I permitted what people consider cruel because their selfish self-centeredness has deprived them of light and thus keeps them from knowing my truth. But if they would be willing to lift the cloud they would know my truth and love it, and thus they would hold all things in reverence and at harvest time they would reap the fruit of their labors.

The Dialogue, 139

Blessed John Ruusbroec (1293-1381), *the Flemish mystic, uniquely synthesized Greek spiritual theology with Augustinian introspection and became one of the most outstanding of all the mystical writers who made the fourteenth century unique. In this passage John shows the humility of Mary and how Christ in the washing of the feet exemplified humility of service.*

When Mary conceived our Lord, she was chaste, pure, and virginal, full of God's grace. She was also knowledgeable and wise in the way she questioned and answered the angel, who taught her the complete truth. She was humble to the core of her being, a quality which drew the Son of God from heaven to our earthly valley. And she said: *I am the handmaid of the Lord and it is his will which I must desire. Let it be done to me according to your word.* When the Holy Spirit heard these words, they were so pleasing to God's own love that the Spirit sent God's Son into Mary's womb, the Son who freed us from every evil.

Now note what follows and learn from it. Although Mary was chosen above all creatures to be the mother of God and the queen of heaven and earth, she nevertheless chose to be the handmaid of God and of all the world. Therefore, when she had conceived our Lord, she went with great haste into the hill country to serve Saint Elizabeth, the mother of Saint John the Baptist, as her humble handmaid until the time when Saint John was born. In the same way her Son, our dear Lord Jesus Christ, who is both divine and human, after he had consecrated the blessed sacrament, given it to his disciples, and received it himself, wrapped a linen towel around himself, knelt before his disciples, washed their feet, and dried them with the towel.　　*A Mirror of Eternal Blessedness II*

In the fifteenth century **Julian of Norwich** *(d.1423), an anchoress and a mystic, was a very well-educated and devout woman. Her book* Showings *reveals her visions and her deep insights into life with God, whom she at times refers to as Mother. In this passage she shows how Mary is a model of strength for all who do God's will.*

Our Lord Jesus brought our Lady Saint Mary to my understanding. I saw her spirituality in her bodily likeness, a simple, humble maiden, young in years, grown a little taller than a child, of the stature which she had when she conceived. Also God showed me part of the wisdom and the truth of her soul, and in this I understood the reverent contemplation with which she beheld her God, who is her Creator, marveling with great reverence that he was willing to be born of her who was a simple creature created by him. And this wisdom and truth, this knowledge of her Creator's greatness and of her own created littleness, made her say very meekly to Gabriel: Behold me here, God's handmaiden. In this sight I understood truly that she is greater, more worthy and more fulfilled than everything else which God has created, and which is inferior to her. Above her is no created thing, except the blessed humanity of Christ, as I saw.

Showings chapter 4

Our good Lord showed to us our Lady Saint Mary to signify the exalted wisdom and truth which were hers as she contemplated her Creator. This wisdom and truth showed her in contemplation how great, how exalted, how mighty and how good was her God. The greatness and nobility of her contemplation of God filled her full of reverent fear; and with this she saw herself so small and so humble, so simple and so poor in comparison with her God that this reverent fear filled her with humility. And founded on this, she was filled with grace and with every kind of virtue, and she surpasses all creatures.   *Showings chapter* 7

In the same time that God joined himself to our body in the maiden's womb, he took our soul, which is sensual, and in taking it, having enclosed us all in himself, he united to our substance. In this union he was perfect man, for Christ, having joined in himself every man who will be saved, is perfect man. So our Lady is our mother, in whom we are all enclosed and born of her in Christ, for she who is mother of our savior is mother of all who are saved in our savior; and our savior is our true Mother, in whom we are endlessly born and out of whom we shall never come.

Showings chapter 57

The Reformers' Movement

The sixteenth century was a difficult era for the Church. Theology was in decline; abuses faced the Church everywhere. Sentimentality and superstition infiltrated religious thought to the extreme. The reformers disassociated themselves from marian devotion so much so that Luther could say in 1523: "I desire that the cult of Mary be totally abandoned solely because of the abuses which arise from it."

The devotees of Mary reacted to the contempt and hostility of the reformers. For this reason the sixteenth century becomes one of the richest periods of marian writings — a period which is the backbone for marian devotion from now to the twentieth century.

Dionisio Vazquez (1479-1529), an Augustinian friar who preached both at the papal court in Rome and at the imperial court in Spain, was the forerunner of several great Spanish preachers of this century — Thomas of Villanova, Juan de Avila, and Alfonso de Orozco. In this passage he highlights the role of Mary's motherhood at the birth of Jesus and at the death of Jesus.

We have Saint Augustine's authority for calling this feast of the resurrection a second birth of Christ. The Saint says that Christ had two births. The first occurred when he was born from the matchless virginal womb of Mary, for there has not been and never will be another of comparable virginity. This first birth was truly a birth. The second birth occurred when Christ emerged from the tomb and was a metaphorical birth. He thus dwelt in two unique wombs, for the womb of the sepulcher was as unique in its own way as the Virgin's womb was in its way.

In this second birth the Mother of God, who had ceased to be a mother, was again chosen to be Mother of God.

Let us go a step further and see which feast was more fully hers: the feast of the resurrection or the feast of the nativity. Truly, the former was much more hers! At the nativity she truly became the Mother of God because she gave birth to him; at the resurrection, however, she became the Mother of God by recovering what she had lost.

At the nativity she became a mother who would cease to be a mother; at the resurrection she became a mother who would not again cease to be a mother. At the nativity she became mother of a man who must some day cease to be a man; at the resurrection she became mother of a man forever incorruptible. Bless my soul! How much a feast of Mary this is! How much, indeed!

Let us congratulate her, therefore, for becoming a mother by that first birth; with even greater joy let us congratulate her for becoming Mother of God as well as man. And yet we look for much greater and more abundant blessings from this second birth in which you see the most exalted mother who ever has or ever will exist! Lady, until this point we called you Mother only conditionally; henceforth we shall call you Mother without reservation. And since the blessings we look for cannot be gained without grace, grant us a little of it, Lady, for you are in a position to win it for us. And to put you under a greater obligation, we recite the antiphon with which the entire Church greets you today: "Queen of heaven, rejoice. . . ."

Sermon on the Resurrection

Saint Thomas More (1477-1535), *chancellor in the court of Henry VIII of England, was beheaded by order of the king whom he had resisted in the matter of his divorce. In this passage which comes from one of his many writings, Saint Thomas More writes, in the English of his time, how Mary remained with faith when all others had lost it.*

But since that upon Saint Peter's first confession of the right faith that Christ was God's son, our Lord made him his universal vicar and under him head of his Church, and that for his successor he should be the first upon whom and whose firm confessed faith he would build his Church and of any that was only man make him the first and chief head and ruler thereof, therefore he showed him that his faith, that is to say the faith by him confessed, should never fail in his Church, nor never did it, notwithstanding his denying. For yet stood still the light of faith in Our Lady, of whom we read in the gospel continual assistance to her sweetest son without fleeing or flitting. And in all other we find either fleeing from him one time or another, or else doubt of his resurrection after his death, his dear mother only except, for the signification and remembrance whereof the Church yearly in the Tenebrae lessons leaveth her candle burning still when all the remnant, that signifieth his apostles and disciples, be one by one put out. And since his faith in effect failed, and yet the faith that he professed abode still in Our Lady, the promise that God made was, as it seemeth, meant to him but as head of the Church.   *A Book for All Seasons, December 15*

Saint Thomas of Villanova (1486-1555), *an Augustinian
bishop, dedicated himself to preaching, reform, and caring for the
poor. He puts the fruits of his own contemplation at the service of his
flock. His many sermons are replete with beautiful marian expressions.
In this passage he reflects on the mystery of the annunciation.*

Our minds cannot grasp what took place in Mary
when she had spoken the words: *Let it be done to me as
you say.* For as soon as these words were spoken, *the
Word was made flesh.* By the action of the Holy Spirit
the holy body of the Lord was formed in an instant
from her pure blood and in that same instant organ-
ized and ensouled and united to the Word of God.
The child was immediately filled with every grace and
virtue, endowed with all the charisms, beatified by the
clear vision of God, and, finally, enriched with all the
wisdom, grace, and glory he now enjoys in heaven.
"For there is no force that can delay the grace of the
Holy Spirit," as Ambrose says, nor does the skilled
Spirit need time for his work.

O utterly astounding conception! O sacred womb!
O womb of utmost purity, dwelling of the divinity,
sanctuary of the Spirit, conveyance of the divine
Word, triumphal chariot of the eternal King, and
carriage of the true Solomon, for as it is written: *I
compare you, my love, to a mare of Pharaoh's chariots.* O
womb wider than the heavens, brighter than the
empyrean, more fragrant than paradise! For this is the
true paradise of human beings, the place where God
first deigned to make himself visible to humankind.

Who can describe the delights of this womb? Who can worthily expound its riches? I beg you, Virgin: tell us yourself how you conceived with your virginity unimpaired and gave birth with your virginity intact. Tell us your feelings as you were wholly bathed in the sweet nectar of the divinity; as you embraced that limitless ocean of pleasure in so narrow a vessel and knew for certain that the delight of the human race was contained within you. Tell us, what fire burned in you, what flames leapt up, as the furnace that is God descended into your tender womb and the abyss of sweetness thrust itself into this compact abdomen? Tell us, blessed one, what dense masses of sweetness did that endlessly flowing fountain gush forth as it was hemmed in by the narrow womb? What burning sparks did that conflagration scatter as it was covered by the veil of flesh? What rays did that brightest of suns send forth when covered by so thin a little cloud? Tell us, holy Virgin, flower and glory of virgins, what power enabled you to withstand such intense on-slaughts of delight? What impulses, what waves of passionate love did you sustain?

O God-bearing Ark, filled with great pleasure! O most beautiful of vessels, filled with heavenly balsam! What praises can I utter to exalt you? O Virgin, how my powers lag and my eloquence fails me in the face of your excellence, your bliss, your sublimity, and your glory! For whatever we think or say of you falls utterly short of the praise you deserve and is utterly outstripped by your blessedness. For in a single flight you were raised to so high a dignity that no human or even angelic eye can reach you in your lofty place. In an instant a daughter of Adam, a lowly girl became Mother of the creator, Mistress of the world, Queen of heaven, and Empress of all creation!

Annunciation of the Blessed Virgin Mary, Sermon II, 5-7

Martin Luther (1483-1546), *like his contemporary Saint Thomas of Villanova, was also a champion for much needed reform within the Church, but he had drawn upon himself the logical consequences of his theology with his break from, and later excommunication by, Rome. For Luther, scripture and Saint Augustine were his two companions; it is within this vein that he wrote one of his greatest works (in 1520 before his final break with Rome), the Magnificat. In it he shows his true filial devotion to the Mother of God.*

Mary confesses that the foremost work God did for her was that he regarded her, which is indeed the greatest of his works, on which all the rest depend and from which they all derive. For where it comes to pass that God turns his face toward one to regard him, there is nothing but grace and salvation, and all gifts and works must follow. Thus we read in Genesis that he had regard for Abel and his offering, but for Cain and his offering he had no regard. Here is the origin of the many prayers in the psalter — that God would lift up his countenance upon us, that he would not hide his countenance from us, that he would make his face shine upon us, and the like. And that Mary herself regards this as the chief thing, she indicates by saying: *Behold, since he has regarded me, all generations will call me blessed.*

Note that she does not say people will speak all manner of good of her, praise her virtues, exalt her virginity or her humility, or sing of what she has done. But for this one thing alone, that God regarded her, people will call her blessed. That is to give all the glory to God as completely as it can be done. Therefore she points to God's regard and says: *For, behold, henceforth all generations will call me blessed.*

Mary confesses that the foremost work God did for her was that he regarded her, which is indeed the greatest of his works, on which all the rest depend and from which they all derive. For where it comes to pass that God turns his face toward one to regard him, there is nothing but grace and salvation, and all gifts and works must follow. Thus we read in Genesis that he had regard for Abel and his offering, but for Cain and his offering he had no regard. Here is the origin of the many prayers in the psalter — that God would lift up his countenance upon us, that he would not hide his countenance from us, that he would make his face shine upon us, and the like. And that Mary herself regards this as the chief thing, she indicates by saying: *Behold, since he has regarded me, all generations will call me blessed.*

Note that she does not say people will speak all manner of good of her, praise her virtues, exalt her virginity or her humility, or sing of what she has done. But for this one thing alone, that God regarded her, people will call her blessed. That is to give all the glory to God as completely as it can be done. Therefore she points to God's regard and says: *For, behold, henceforth all generations will call me blessed. That is, beginning with the time when God regarded my low estate, I shall be called blessed.* Not *she* is praised thereby, but God's *grace* toward her. In fact, she is despised, and she despises herself in that she says her low estate was regarded by God. Therefore she also mentions her blessedness before enumerating the works that God did to her, and ascribes it all to the fact that God regarded her low estate.

131

Martin Luther

For he who is mighty has done great things for me, and holy is his name. The *great things* are nothing less than that she became the Mother of God, in which work so many and such great good things are bestowed on her as pass man's understanding. For on this there follows all honor, all blessedness, and her unique place in the whole of humankind, among which she has no equal, namely, that she had a child by the Father in heaven, and such a child. She herself is unable to find a name for this work, it is too exceedingly great; all she can do is break out in the fervent cry: "They are great things," impossible to describe or define. Hence men and women have crowned all her glory into a single word, calling her the Mother of God. No one can say anything greater of her or to her, though he had as many tongues as there are leaves on the trees, or grass in the fields, or stars in the sky, or sand by the sea. It needs to be pondered in the heart what it means to be the Mother of God.

Mary also freely ascribes all to God's grace, not to her merit. For though she was without sin, yet that grace was far too great for her to deserve it in any way. How should a creature deserve to become the Mother of God? Though certain scribblers make much ado about her worthiness for such motherhood, I prefer to believe her rather than them. She says her low estate was regarded by God, not thereby rewarding her for anything she had done, but, *he has done great things for me,* he has done this of his own accord without any doing of mine.

Magnificat 48-49

Venerable Thomas of Jesus (1529-1582) *wrote the book* The Sufferings of Jesus, *a work which has guided many people on their path to holiness. Saint Elizabeth Ann Seton of the United States was influenced by this book. While in prison in Africa and ministering to his fellow prisoners, this Augustinian Friar wrote this classical life of Jesus. In it he speaks of the Mother of Jesus and her sufferings as a result of her yes to the mystery of the Word made flesh.*

None but the two hearts of the Mother and Son can conceive the whole of their sufferings because, the measure of their pain being that of their love, to know what they suffered we must know how much they loved; and we are very far from that knowledge because we are very far from their love. Let each of us, therefore, according to the degree of our enlightenment and charity, endeavor rather to enter into their feelings than to try to express them in words.

Though it would seem that nothing could be added to the Blessed Virgin's afflicted state, yet her sorrowful heart still received from time to time fresh wounds resulting from different circumstances of her Son's passion. Such circumstances were when she heard him cry out: *My God, my God, why have you forsaken me?* When she saw him offered gall and vinegar to quench the burning thirst of which he complained. When he sent forth that loud cry when he expired. When she received him dead in her arms after he had been taken down from the cross. When he was buried; and when she saw herself deprived of the presence of her loved One whose resurrection she desired so ardently that those three days seemed to her like three years.

It must not be doubted but that the pains of his holy Mother, whom he beheld at the foot of the cross, were more severe to him than the pains he suffered on the cross itself. For that most pure Virgin was worthier of his love than all the angels of heaven, and all the creatures on earth, and consequently was loved more. No mother had ever loved a child more ardently or more tenderly, she had been the faithful companion of his labors, was holy and innocent, deserved not to suffer any pain because she had never been defiled by sin, and yet of all mothers who had gone before her, and were to come after her, she was the most afflicted. Let us imagine, if we can, what pain it must have been for such a mother to see such a Son expire in the midst of so many torments and insults. So severe a cross was reserved for her alone because she alone was capable of bearing it. It is true that our Savior, out of the respect he had for his mother, did not allow the executioners to ill-treat her, but the love she bore her Son caused her more torments than anything the executioners might have done to her.

Jesus took care of her, spoke to her, gave her for a son the disciple he loved, and said to that disciple, *Behold your mother.* As Saint John here represented all peoples, our Savior commanded us all in his person to honor and serve the Blessed Virgin as our Mother. It was, nevertheless, a great consolation to that afflicted Mother to hear the voice of her only Son. She knew that by adopting a second son she ceased not to be the mother of the first, whom she regarded as her Creator and her God. The holy Virgin accepted Saint John as her son in the same way as she accepted, at the same time, all the human race as her children. She accepted this trust because she clearly saw that it was the will of Christ, and that men, after having treated him so badly, would never presume to return to him if he did not give them his own Mother to act as a mediatrix.

She entered fully into her Son's intentions, assumed the heart of a mother for all sinners, and looked upon them as the children of sorrow whom she had brought forth at the foot of the cross. Thus that sea of sufferings into which Jesus and Mary were plunged has become for sinners a river of peace and a fountain of blessings. Let us, therefore, have our eyes continually fixed on these models of perfection, let us consecrate to their service the remainder of our lives, let us endeavor to tread in their footsteps, and let us realize that in order to be agreeable to God we must become like Jesus and Mary. *The Sufferings of Jesus, chapter 47*

Blessed Alfonso de Orozco (1500-1591), *an Augustinian friar, was a famous preacher at the court of Spain. He also wrote much on the spiritual life and became known for his contribution to the literature of the Golden Age of Spain. In his book on marian homilies he reflects on Mary's reply and her humility.*

Behold the handmaid of the Lord. Be it done to me as you say. What splendid words, and how efficacious and fruitful! The Word was immediately made flesh and dwelt among us. As soon as the Blessed Virgin spoke, the Holy Spirit exerted his power: he formed the most holy body of Christ, created his soul, and united our humanity to the Word of God. An agent whose power is infinite can in an instant dispose matter to receive its due form, as Saint Thomas says. The blessed body of Christ then grew because his soul exercised its power of increase; his soul is of the same species as ours, and therefore his body was bound to grow in the same manner as ours. This happened so that our Savior might be clearly seen to have a genuine human nature.

Behold the handmaid of the Lord. Be it done to me as you say. It is as if she were saying: I am a painter's canvas; let the almighty painter draw as he wishes and do as he pleases. How marvelous that when she learns this to be the Holy Spirit's work, she asks no more questions but immediately holds herself ready! Even more astonishing: on hearing herself exalted to the position of mother of the Messiah she takes refuge in the citadel of humility and acknowledges herself to be a handmaid and describes herself as such! In short, not only does she give consent, but she adds a prayer: *Be it done to me as you say.*

Brethren, what astounding power was contained in this "fiat" of the Virgin! This is the word by which God created light and the heavens: *Let there be light,* and there was light; *Let the firmament be made,* and the firmament was made. But when the gracious Virgin said *fiat,* the Word was made flesh! See how much more excellent and astonishing is the work accomplished through the "fiat" of his Mother. Truly, the incarnation of God surpasses the entire creation of the world. Who is not struck dumb on hearing of it? Who is so untutored as not to be rapt in wonder?

I think it worthwhile to search out the many rare and wonderful virtues which the Virgin Mother of God has proposed for our imitation in her words to the angel. *Behold the handmaid of the Lord,* says the holy Virgin, and displays, above all else, humility, obedience, and love for us.

Her great humility shines out when she calls herself a handmaid. Of all the virtues of the Virgin the most admirable is her great humility; it is a virtue of which we ourselves have great need. Which of us, I ask you, is disturbed by acclaim? Which of us is not buoyed up at hearing his own praises sung? Which of us is not exalted and lifted above himself when he hears himself praised? How far we are from the Virgin's modesty! We are transported when others praise us falsely; Mary was disturbed when the angel praised her truthfully, and she ended by calling herself a handmaid.

Declamationes 4, pages 84-87

Luis de Léon (1527-1591), *an Augustinian friar, was a poet, mystic, scriptural scholar, and theologian. Above all he was a holy person who suffered much for his beliefs. He was editor of the works of Saint Teresa of Jesus of Avila, and probably on account of him her works and spirituality are available to us today. His most precious work is a poem to Mary. In his famous work* The Names of Christ *he acknowledges that he is under Mary's protection.*

As unto heaven thou'rt soaring,
O Queen, to blissful lays,
Take thou my soul imploring
Thy mantle's hem, and raise
Me to those Hills of Praise!

The choiring angels round thee
Attend as from thy birth;
With stars their hands have crowned thee
Of more than queenly worth –
Thou treadst the moon as earth!

But turn thine eyes, O Tender,
O Loving – ere dost leave
This vale whose flowery splendor
Masks but a waste where grieve
Thine exiled sons of Eve.

So why thy gentle vision
hath marked our dismal plight,
Thou on thy way elysian
Mayst trail us in thy flight –
Heaven's lode – star to the light!

Virgin of virgins,
you were untouched by that stain of sin,
that first of all evils,
the sad inheritance of the human race.
From my earliest years
I have placed my hope in you.
Where the power of evil overcomes me
and makes my life too sinful for your gaze,
all the more will your unbounded compassion
show me your generous love,
because my suffering is so deep,
my sinfulness so unworthy of your aid.

Poems

"Now I am even more content, Marcelo, having called to your mind what you forgot, because I am delighted to hear you say that the principle of virginal purity and integrity in our common Mother and Lady is specified in ancient letters and prophecy. Reason demands it. When they said and wrote so many things of less importance, it was not possible to silence such a great mystery. If other references appear which belong to it, and they surely will present themselves, I would be very happy if you state them, if it does not bore you."

"In no way," Marcelo replied, "does it bore me to say something in praise of my unique advocate and Lady. Although she belongs to everyone, I dare call her my Lady and my particular advocate because from childhood I put myself completely under her protection."

The Names of Christ, Book I

Saint John of the Cross (1542-1591), *a Carmelite friar, who was persuaded by Saint Teresa of Jesus of Avila to undertake the reform of his Order, which cost him much hard work and many trials, was outstanding in holiness and knowledge and considered a mystic. He too wrote about Mary's role in salvation history.*

> Then he called
> The archangel Gabriel
> And sent him to
> The virgin Mary,
>
> At whose consent
> The mystery was wrought,
> In whom the Trinity
> Clothed the Word with flesh.
>
> And though Three work this,
> It is wrought in the One:
> And the Word lived incarnate
> In the womb of Mary.
>
> And He who had only a Father
> Now had a Mother too,
> But she was not like others
> Who conceive by man.
>
> From her own flesh
> He received His flesh,
> So He is called
> Son of God and of man.
>
> *Poetry, Romance 8*

The Dogma of the Immaculate Conception
Second Phase

In the seventeenth and eighteenth centuries the blossoming of a tremendous specialized marian literature occurred; it will meet its culminating point in the last half of the nineteenth century.

Cardinal Pierre de Bérulle (1575-1629), *statesman and reformer, worked hard in implementing the decrees of the Council of Trent, especially with regard to priestly formation. In imitation of the Oriental school of expression, he speaks much of the mystery of the incarnation and Mary as mother and God as Father. In this passage Mary's silence is depicted as a silence of praise.*

It falls to the Virgin to keep silence. It is her condition, her road, her life. Her life is a life of silence, which adores the eternal Word. Seeing before her eyes, at her breast, in her arms, this same Word, the substantial Word of the Father, to be dumb and reduced to silence by the condition of his childhood, she enters again into a new silence and is transformed by it after the example of the incarnate Word who is her Son, her God, and her sole love. And in that way her life goes on, from silence to silence, from a silence of adoration to a silence of transformation.

Mary is in silence, enraptured by the silence of her Son Jesus. One of the sacred and divine effects of the silence of Jesus is to put the most holy Mother of Jesus into a life of silence: a silence that is humble, profound, and that adores the incarnate Wisdom with more holiness and eloquence than the words of either angels or humans. This silence on the part of the Virgin is not a silence of one who hesitates in speech or one who is helpless: it is a silence more eloquent in its praise of Jesus than eloquence itself.

And so it is marvelous to see that, in this condition of silence and the childhood of Jesus, everyone speaks and Mary says nothing at all.   *Opuscules de piete, 39*

Bartolomé de los Rios (1580-1652), *an Augustinian friar from Spain and an eloquent preacher, propagated the Confraternity of the Slaves of Mary to the Low Countries. From there it spread to France, Germany, Italy, Poland, and other parts; in 1631 Pope Urban VIII gave offical approbation to the confraternity. Father Bartolome wrote much on this notion; his monumental work is* Hierarchia Mariana.

Virgin of virgins,
I choose you today
as my sovereign, my queen, my empress,
and I declare myself, as I am in fact,
your servant and your slave.
I invoke your royal name of Mary,
that is, sovereign Lady,
and beg of you with all my heart
to admit me into the privileged circle of your family
as one of your servants,
to do your will
as a humble slave and loving child.
As a sign of your acceptance
engrave on my heart with the fire of your love
not the brand of an unwilling slave,
but those two gracious words of the angel:
Ave Maria.

As long as I draw breath
may your burning love ensure
that I bear these words
in my heart and in my memory,
and that until my dying breath
my will may be always on fire
with my great desire to serve you,
my sovereign and my Queen,
glorious in your majesty.

Though I am in every way unworthy
of so honorable a title,
I resolve sincerely to be your slave,
to serve you wholeheartedly,
to protect your name,
and that of your Son,
against every insult,
as far as it may rest with me,
and never to allow anyone in my charge
to offend your Son in any way.
By your tender love for your Son,
by the glories you have received
from the Most Holy Trinity,
do not reject me from your service
but as my sovereign and my Queen
preside over all my actions,
command whatever you will,
direct all my work,
remedy all its defects.

During my whole life
rule over me
as your servant and slave.
At the hour of my death,
as I hope for
at the end of my loving servitude
among the privileged members of your family,
receive my soul
and escort it
into the presence of God.

Hierarchia Mariana

Jacques Bossuet (1627-1704), *outstanding Churchman and orator, was prepared for ordination by Saint Vincent de Paul. Bossuet became a famous preacher and educator. As bishop of Metz he preached to his people; he also wrote several treatises for the religious; his many sermons have been preserved. He had an ardent devotion to the Blessed Mother. In this sermon he reflects on Mary and Elizabeth's embrace and sees in it the fulfillment of Christianity.*

Although the gospel and the law might perhaps seem to be far apart, yet we know there is nothing more completely united, and that Jesus Christ only came to the world to fulfill the law and the prophets by the truths of his gospel. There is neither full stop nor comma in the law, if I may use such terms, which do not find their real meaning in Jesus Christ alone; and we know that all that Jesus Christ did was solely intended to fulfill exactly and at all points what had been written of him in the law. Thus, however different they may look to us, Moses and Jesus Christ are close to one another; the synagogue and the Church hold out their hands to each other: and when I think of the visit of Mary to Elizabeth and of their embrace, I see the gospel kiss the law, and the Church embrace the synagogue. This is the heart and meaning of the mysterious diversity of this great scene, where Jesus Christ goes to Saint John and Mary visits Saint Elizabeth; where a child leaps for joy, his mother prophesies, and a Virgin breaks into thanksgiving.

Mary and Elizabeth embrace. They greet one another. The law honors the gospel in foretelling it; the gospel honors the law in fulfilling it: this is their greeting to one another. Let us listen now to their holy conversation. *You are blessed above all women.* You, the Church, the community of the faithful, an assembly dear above all communities on earth, you are singularly blessed because you have been uniquely chosen. *My dove is one, my perfect one. You are blessed because you have believed,* Elizabeth says to Mary; and rightly, since faith is the source of every grace: *For the righteous live by faith. All that the Lord has told you will be accomplished.* All will be accomplished: that is the meaning of the Christian life. Christians are children of a promise, children of hope: that is the witness the synagogue bears to the Church. The Church does not disown her gifts or advantages; on the contrary, she acknowledges that *the Almighty has done great things in her.* But she gives the praise to God: *My soul glorifies the Lord.* Thus it happens in this kindly meeting of the synagogue with the Church, that while the synagogue, as it must, bears faithful witness to the Church, the Church for her part bears witness to the divine mercy, to teach us Christians that the true sacrifice of the new law is the sacrifice of thanksgiving.

Sermons: Volume 4, pages 268-269

Saint Louis-Marie Grignion de Montfort (1673-1716) *is widely known for his promotion of marian devotion with his famous book* True Devotion to Mary. *His devotion is christocentric, despite criticisms to the opposite, and although he does expound the notion of slavery toward Jesus through Mary — a notion already prevalent in Bartolome de los Rios, who had a great influence on him, he uses this notion as freedom from bondage of sin and the world.*

The totus tuus *(All for you — meaning Mary) aspect comes originally from Saint Bonaventure but de Montfort is the one who spread it. Pope John Paul II has taken* totus tuus *for his own marian spirituality.*

Saint Bernard says: "Since you were unworthy to receive the divine graces, they were given to Mary, so that whatever you would have, you would receive through her." God, says Saint Bernard, seeing that we are unworthy to receive his graces immediately from his own hand, gives them to Mary, in order that we may have through her whatever he wills to give us; and he also finds his glory in receiving, through the hands of Mary, the gratitude, respect, and love which we owe him for his benefits. It is most just, then, that we imitate this conduct of God, in order, as the same Saint Bernard says, that grace return to its author by the same channel through which it came: "That grace should return to the given by the same channel through which it came."

This is precisely what our devotion does. We offer and consecrate all we are and all we have to the Blessed Virgin, in order that our Lord may receive through her mediation the glory and the gratitude which we owe him. We acknowledge ourselves unworthy and unfit to approach his infinite Majesty by ourselves; and it is on this account that we avail ourselves of the intercession of the most holy Virgin.

Moreover, this devotion is a practice of great humility, which God loves above all the other virtues. A soul which exalts itself abases God; a soul which abases itself exalts God. God resists the proud and gives his grace to the humble. If you abase yourself, thinking yourself unworthy to appear before him and to draw nigh to him, he descends and lowers himself to come to you, to take pleasure in you, and to exalt you in spite of yourself. On the contrary, when you are not bold enough to approach God without a mediator, God flies from you and you cannot reach him. Oh, how he loves humility of heart! It is to this humility that this devotion induces us, because it teaches us never to draw nigh, of ourselves, to our Lord, however sweet and merciful he may be, but always to avail ourselves of the intercession of our Blessed Lady, whether it be to appear before God, or to speak to him, or to draw near to him, or to offer him anything, or to unite and consecrate ourselves to him.

The most holy Virgin, who is a Mother of sweetness and mercy, and who never lets herself be outdone in love and liberality, seeing that we give ourselves entirely to her, to honor and to serve her, and for that end strip ourselves of all that is dearest to us in order to adorn her, meets us in the same spirit. She also gives her whole self, and gives it in an unspeakable manner, to him who gives all to her. She causes him to be engulfed in the abyss of her graces. She adorns him with her merits; she supports him with her power; she illuminates him with her light; she inflames him with her love; she communicates to him her virtues, her humility, her faith, her purity, and the rest. She makes herself his bail, his supplement, and his dear all toward Jesus. In a word, as that consecrated person is all Mary's, so Mary is all his; after such a fashion that we can say of that perfect servant and child of Mary what Saint John the Evangelist said of himself, that he took the holy Virgin for his own: *The disciple took her for his own.*

It is this which produces in the soul, if it is faithful, a great distrust, contempt, and hatred of self, and a great confidence in and self-abandonment to the Blessed Virgin, its good Mistress.

A man no longer, as before, relies on his own dispositions, intentions, merits, virtues, and good works; because having made an entire sacrifice of them to Jesus Christ by that good Mother, he has but one treasure now, where all his goods are laid up, and that is no longer in himself, for his treasure is Mary.

That is what makes him approach our Lord without servile or scrupulous fear, and pray to him with great confidence. This is what makes him share the sentiments of the devout and learned Abbot Rupert, who, alluding to the victory that Jacob gained over the angel, said to our Blessed Lady these beautiful words: "O Mary, my Princess, Immaculate Mother of the God-Man, Jesus Christ, I desire to wrestle with that man, namely, the Divine Word, not armed with my own merits but with yours."

Oh, how strong and mighty we are with Jesus Christ, when we are armed with the merits and intercession of the worthy Mother of God, who, as Saint Augustine says, has lovingly vanquished the Most High.

True Devotion to Mary 141-145

In the mid-seventeenth century a notable Irish Augustinian literary figure, **Fergal Dubh (Black) O'Gara,**[1] was a refugee from the Cromwellian persecution. While in the Low Countries he compiled a collection of bardic Irish poems which is justly renowned as a source book on Gaelic poetry. The poems cover the years 1060-1630. A wistful marginal note by O'Gara runs: "12th February at Lille in the Low Countries, 1656. Here I break off until morning and in gloom and grief. Yes and so to be during my life's length unless I think that I might have one look at Ireland. Fergal O'Gara of the Augustinian Order." Fortunately in the preface, which was added later, he has the note "and now I am safe and sound back at Banada in Ireland, 5 June 1686." Banada was a well-known Augustinian monastery of the Observant reform movement to which the Augustinians returned after the Cromwellian persecution. The verses he wrote while in exile were:

19 July 1657

Praise to God,
to the most glorious Virgin Mary,
and to all the Saints.

1657

Most happy among women;
A Woman among women;
A Mother among mothers;
A Virgin among virgins;

Mary Immaculate, the ever-Virgin,
To whom be praise and honor for ever and ever,
And also to our Holy Saint Augustine.

---

1. I am indebted to F.X. Martin, O.S.A., for the information on this person.

At the close of this century **Saint Alphonsus Liguori** *(1697-1787) wrote eloquently about Mary in his book* The Glories of Mary. *His theme is the submission of the Son of God to his parents and the essential submission of Mary to the Creator in her yes.*

It is true that Jesus now in heaven sits at the right hand of the Father, that is, as Saint Thomas explains it, even as man, on account of the hypostatical union with the person of the divine Word. He has supreme dominion over all, and also over Mary; it will nevertheless be always true that for a time, when he was living in this world, he was pleased to humble himself and to be subject to Mary, as we are told by Saint Luke: *And he was subject to them.* And still more, says Saint Ambrose, Jesus Christ having deigned to make Mary his mother, inasmuch as he was her Son, he was truly obliged to obey her. And for this reason, says Richard of Saint Laurence, "of other saints we say that they are with God; but of Mary alone can it be said that she was so far favored as to be not only herself submissive to the will of God, but even that God was subject to her will." And whereas of all other virgins, remarks the same author, we must say that *they follow the Lamb whithersoever he goes,* of the Blessed Virgin Mary we can say that the Lamb followed her, having become subject to her.

And here we say, that although Mary, now in heaven, can no longer command her Son, nevertheless her prayers are always the prayers of a Mother, and consequently most powerful to obtain whatever she asks.

The Glories of Mary, Part I, chapter 6, I, 2

Mary, Mother of the Church
The Immaculate Conception

The dogmatic definition of the Immaculate Conception (*Ineffabilis Deus*) was proclaimed by Pope Pius IX on 8 December 1854:

> To the honor of the holy and undivided Trinity, to the glory and adornment of the Virgin Mother of God, to the exaltation of the Catholic faith and the increase of the Christian religion, we, by the authority of Jesus Christ our Lord, of the blessed apostles, Peter and Paul, and by our own, declare, pronounce, and define that the doctrine, which holds that the most Blessed Virgin Mary at the first instant of her conception, by a singular grace and privilege of Almighty God, in consideration of the merits of Jesus Christ, the Savior of the human race, was preserved free from all stain of original sin, has been revealed by God, and therefore is to be firmly and constantly believed by all the faithful.

Through the writings of the centuries preceding this definition we have seen how many already articulated this belief. Even Pope Pius IX used the formula of Alexander VII of 8 December 1661.

During the nineteenth century the month of May dedicated to Mary began to take hold and there were apparitions on 19 September 1846 at La Salette, France. The apparitions of Lourdes, France, took place from 1858 onward. Since then there has ever been interest in the apparitions of Mary, the Mother of God.

On 1 November 1950 Pope Pius XII defined the dogma of the Assumption of Mary to heavenly glory. During the Second Vatican Council Pope Paul VI hailed Mary as Mother of the Church. Devotion to Mary continues.

Pope Pius IX (1792-1878), one of the longest reigning popes of history, had a very turbulent pontificate. On 8 December 1854 he proclaimed the dogma of the Immaculate Conception of Mary. This doctrine was written and preached about for centuries. After the proclamation he speaks tenderly about the Blessed Mother and her role toward us.

Let all the children of the Catholic Church who are most dear to us hear our words, and with even more ardent zeal for piety, religion, and love, continue to cherish, invoke, and beseech the Blessed Virgin Mary, Mother of God, conceived without original sin, and let them with entire confidence have recourse to this sweetest Mother of grace and mercy in all dangers, difficulties, necessities, doubts, and fears. For nothing need be feared, and nothing need be despaired of, so long as she is our guide, our patroness, so long as she is propitious, she our protectress. Surely, she who bears toward us the affection of a mother, and who through her interest in the affairs of all humankind is solicitous for our salvation, and who has been appointed by the Lord as Queen of heaven and earth, and has been exalted above all the choirs of the angels and ranks of the saints, surely she, standing at the right hand of her only begotten Son, our Lord Jesus Christ, and with a mother's prayer, is most influential in her intercession, and obtains what she asks and cannot be denied.

Acta 1, 607-618

Cardinal John Henry Newman (1801-1890), *a great church-man in his time, lives on today through his example and his writings. In his many sermons he speaks of Mary. In this selection he talks about Mary's recompense as the Mother of God.*

Now, as you know, it has been held from the first, and defined from an early age, that Mary is the Mother of God. She is not merely the Mother of our Lord's manhood, or of our Lord's body, but she is to be considered the Mother of the Word himself, the Word incarnate. God, in the person of the Word, the Second Person of the All-glorious Trinity, took the substance of his human flesh from her, and clothed in it he lay within her; and he bore it about with him after birth, as a sort of badge and witness that he, though God, was hers. He was nursed and tended by her; he was suckled by her; he lay in her arms. As time went on, he ministered to her, and obeyed her. He lived with her for thirty years, in one house, with an uninterrupted intercourse, and with only the saintly Joseph to share it with him. She was the witness of his growth, of his joys, of his sorrows, of his prayers; she was blest with his smile, with the touch of his hand, with the whisper of his affection, with the expression of his thoughts and his feelings for that length of time. Now, my brethren, what ought she to be, what is it *becoming* that she should be, who was so favored?

Such a question was once asked by a heathen king, "What should be done to the man whom the king desireth to honor?" And he received the following answer, "The man whom the king wisheth to honor ought to be clad in the king's apparel, and to be mounted on the king's saddle, and to receive the royal diadem on his head; and let the first among the king's princes and presidents hold his horse, and let him walk through the streets of the city, and say, Thus shall he be honored, whom the king hath a mind to honor." So stands the case with Mary.

I answer, as the king was answered: Nothing is too high for her to whom God owes his human life; no exuberance of grace, no excess of glory but is becoming, but is to be expectd there, where God has lodged himself, whence God has issued. Let her "be clad in the king's apparel," that is, let the fullness of the Godhead so flow into her that she may be a figure of the incommunicable sanctity, and beauty, and glory, of God himself: that she may be the Mirror of Justice, the Mystical Rose, the Tower of Ivory, the House of God, the Morning Star. Let her "receive the king's diadem upon her head," as the Queen of heaven, the Mother of all living, the Health of the weak, the Refuge of sinners, the Comforter of the afflicted. And "let the first amongst the king's princes walk before her," let Angels, and Prophets, and Apostles, and Martyrs, and all Saints kiss the hem of her garment and rejoice under the shadow of her throne.

Discourses Addressed to Mixed Congregations

Blessed Elizabeth of the Trinity (1880-1906), *after a religious life of only five years in the carmel of Dijon, died at the age of twenty-six. However, her spiritual doctrine, which highlighted the indwelling of the Spirit, perpetuated her memory. In this passage Saint Elizabeth emphasizes the interior life of Mary.*

If you knew the gift of God, Christ said one evening to the Samaritan woman. Yet what is this gift of God but himself? *He came to his own home, and his own people received him not,* declared the beloved disciple. To many a soul might Saint John the Baptist utter the reproach: *Among you stands one whom you do not know. If you knew the gift of God!*

There is one created being who did know that gift of God, who lost no particle of it; a creature so pure and luminous that she seemed to be the light itself: mirror of righteousness — a being whose life was so simple, so lost in God, that there is but little to say of it: the faithful Virgin, who *kept all these words in her heart!* She was so lowly, so hidden in God, in the seclusion of the temple, that she drew upon herself the regard of the Holy Trinity: *Because he has regarded the humility of his handmaid, for behold from henceforth all generations shall call me blessed.*

The Father, bending down to this lovely creature, so unaware of her own beauty, chose her for the Mother in time of him whose Father he is in eternity. Then the Spirit of love, who presides over the works of God, overshadowed her; the Virgin uttered her Fiat: *Behold the handmaid of the Lord; be it done to me according to your word,* and the greatest of all mysteries was accomplished. By the descent of the Word into her womb, Mary became God's own for ever and ever.

During the period between the Annunciation and the Nativity, our Lady seems to me to be the model of interior souls: those whom God has called to live within themselves, in the depths of the bottomless abyss. In what peace and recollection did Mary live and act! The most trivial actions were sanctified by her, for through them all, she remained the constant adorer of the gift of God. Yet that did not prevent her from spending herself for others when charity required it. The gospel tells us that *Mary rising up . . . went into the hill country with haste to a city of Judah* to visit her cousin Elizabeth. Never did the ineffable vision which she contemplated within herself lessen her charity for others, because, says one writer, "though contemplation is directed to the praise and the eternity of its Lord, it possesses and will never lose concord."

The Spiritual Doctrine of Elizabeth of the Trinity

Saint Pius X (1835-1914) *as priest, bishop, and pope lived a simple life. The richness of his spirituality is witnessed in his pontificate which was one of restoration. "To restore all things in Christ" was his motto. In this passage he speaks of Mary's role as our mother in this work of restoration.*

Is not Mary the Mother of Christ? She is then our mother too. For everyone should convince himself of this, that Jesus, who is the Word made flesh, is also the savior of the human race. Now, as God-man he acquired, just as others, an individual body. But as restorer of our race, he acquired a spiritual and mystical body — the society of those who believe in Christ. *We, the many, are one body in Christ.* Now, the Virgin conceived the eternal Son of God not only that he might by assuming human nature from her become a man, but that he might, through the nature assumed from her, became as well the savior of mortals. For this reason the angel announced to the shepherds: *Today there is born to you a Savior, who is Christ the Lord.* And thus, in one and the same bosom of his most chaste mother, Christ, at one and the same time, assumed flesh and united to himself a spiritual body which is joined together from those *who were to believe in him.*

In this way, Mary, by bearing the Savior in her womb, can be said to have borne all those whose life was contained in the life of the Savior. All of us, therefore, who are united with Christ and are, as the Apostle says, *members of his body, made from his flesh and bones,* have come forth from the womb of Mary, after the manner of a body that is joined to its head. Hence in a spiritual and mystical sense we are called the children of Mary and she is mother of us all. "Mother indeed in spirit . . . but surely mother of the members of Christ, which we are," Saint Augustine says. If, then, the most Blessed Virgin is at once the Mother of God and the mother of men and women, can anyone doubt that she makes every effort that Christ, *the head of his body, the Church,* should infuse into us, his members, the gifts which are his, in order that we may above all come to know him and to *live by him?*

Encyclical Letter Ad Diem, 1904

John Cuthbert Hedley (1837-1915), *a Benedictine monk and later bishop of Newport, Wales, was widely known for his theological, ascetical, and historical writings. In this passage he praises Mary as the immaculate one.*

The dogma of the Immaculate Conception is one of those bright heavenly streams of revelation which the instinct of a Christian absolutely welcomes with rapture; it finds no obstacles in a heart which has any grasp of the incarnation. For wise reasons, even after Calvary, the mass of men and women were to be born without God's supernatural friendship and without a title to the heaven of the beatific vision. But Christ's Mother was to be born "all holy." As the ancient Fathers say, all the beauty that Christ's blood could give her was hers; she was God's friend, and child, and minister, untouched by the enemy, unstained by the shadow of evil. The spirit of the Immaculate has never been the scene of a battle. It came into existence serene and peaceful as a ship glides in the morning light from the safe harbor into a tranquil sea with a glow upon her sails from the sun which shall never set in all her happy voyage. In her was to be no conflict, no war of the flesh against the spirit. Mary was to walk through the world immaculate — no stain on her purity, no dross in her charity, no obstacle to her love of God. There was in her no barrier to grace. Her immaculate heart was a paradise with an open gate, and the Lord entered in, and her whole will and heart received him.

The Christian Inheritance

Dom Columba Marmion (1858-1923), *a Benedictine monk and abbot of Maredsous, guided many generations in their path to holiness through his spiritual writings. In this passage he shows the impact of Mary's yes.*

God proposes the mystery of the incarnation which will be fulfilled in the Virgin only when she shall have given her free consent. The accomplishment of the mystery hangs in suspense until then. At this moment, according to the saying of Saint Thomas, Mary represents us all in her person. It is as if God awaited the response of the humanity to which he wills to unite himself: *Per annuntiationem expectabatur consensus virginis loco totius humanae naturae,* as Saint Thomas says. What a solemn moment it is! For now the vital mystery of Christianity is about to be decided. And Mary gives her reply: full of faith in the heavenly word, and entirely submissive to the divine will that has just been manifested to her, she says: *Behold the handmaid of the Lord; be it done to me according to your word.* This *fiat* is Mary's consent to the divine plan of redemption; this *fiat* is like the echo of the *fiat* of the creation; but it is a new world, an infinitely higher world, a world of grace that God himself creates after this consent: for at this moment the Divine Word, the second person of the holy Trinity, becomes incarnate in Mary: *And the Word was made flesh.*

Christ, the Life of the Soul, page 345

Anscar Vonier (1875-1938), *a Benedictine monk and abbot of Buckfast Abbey, possessed the gift of expounding abstruse questions so as to make them intelligible not only to professional theologians but to intelligent lay readers as well. He reflects on the motherhoods of Mary and Elizabeth.*

Elizabeth's motherhood may be considered as a term of comparison, to enable us the better to understand and measure the excellency of Mary's motherhood. The gospel of Saint Luke opens with a detailed description of the holiest and purest human motherhood that could possibly be imagined. The evangelist takes pleasure in giving us a full description of the glories of that venerable mother. The arrangement is most perfect, even from the artistic point of view; it is a glorious crescendo, this intertwining of the two motherhoods, that of Elizabeth and that of Mary. When we have read all about Elizabeth's motherhood as described by the pen of Saint Luke, we ask ourselves whether it is possible for a woman to have God nearer to her in the joys of maternity, than it is conveyed by that wonderful proximity of heaven in the origin of John's life. But a greater thing is still to come, a thing that will make a most dramatic appeal to the strongest faith. With Elizabeth's motherhood God's action and grace surround, as with an odor of heavenly life, the laws of created life. With Mary it will be all heavenly life. God's action is not merely the companion of created causality; it is supreme, exclusive, absolutely unconditioned by the created law of life.

This artistic intertwining of the two maternities on the part of the evangelist is a guarantee to us that both maternities were maternities in the full sense of the word. There will always be the danger for our mind to place Mary's divine role in a totally unearthly sphere of things, to think of her motherhood as of something belonging to quite another world. The sublimity of it detracts from its created reality in some careless minds. With Mary's motherhood closely related to Elizabeth's motherhood, we ought to see at once that Mary is truly a mother in the ordinary, real, created mode of maternity. When Elizabeth and Mary met for the first time after the angel's message we have two mothers meeting, one as truly and as really a mother as the other: *And when is this to me, that the Mother of my Lord should come to me?*

Elizabeth's exclamation of joy is also a proclamation of the reality of Mary's motherhood; her own offspring, still hidden in her womb, had leaped for joy at the presence of him who could not be there then in person if Mary's womb were not truly a mother's womb. *Blessed is the fruit of your womb* we have to read in conjunction with that other sentence *The infant in my womb leaped for joy*. Elizabeth, in her tender love for her cousin, keeps the great mystery for us human beings, prevents it from receding into a realm that is no longer man's realm. It was the mission of the Archangel Gabriel to reveal the secrets of the divine maternity; it was Elizabeth's mission to assure us that Mary is as truly a human mother as she is herself.

The Divine Motherhood

Alban Goodier (1869-1939), *a Jesuit and archbishop of Bombay, India, whose scholarly bent, simplicity, and deep piety are revealed in his writings, has had a profound influence on many people in his lifetime and later through his published works. He reflects on Mary as the sorrowful Mother who gave her pledge to the Lord in her reply to the angel.*

Mary had never forgotten what the holy man had said that day when, in accordance with the law, she had offered the child Jesus to the Father in the temple.

She had fled with that child away into a foreign land, with bloodshed in her wake; almost from the first the joy of motherhood had been marred by this agony. Her own child's life had brought death to many children, desolation to many mothers. She had brought him back from exile in fear and trembling, longing to live in Bethlehem, the home of David, but they dared not; hiding at last in Nazareth, the village of no repute, lest evil men might again discover him and seek his life. Once she had lost him for part of three days; the memory of that could never be forgotten, it remained as a warning to her, a foreshadowing, of the greater separation that one day must be. Always she kept it in mind, pondering it in her heart; always she had feared when and how the end would come. This woman of few words but deep understanding had often prayed: *Father, if it be possible, let this chalice pass from me* but not before she had also said: *Behold the handmaid of the Lord. Be it done to me according to your word. Not my will but yours be done.*

The Life of Christ

Emile Mersch (1890-1940), *a Jesuit who during World War II gave his life in heroic sacrifice for others, concentrated his writing on the theology of the mystical body of Christ. He describes Mary's Magnificat.*

The Magnificat is Mary's own song, and when she composed it Jesus was not even born. Yet he made his presence felt to John the Baptist, and more so to her. In Mary's song, his thoughts are uttered: the greatness of the humble, the blessings promised to the lowly, the reversal of values effected by the Lord in exalting the poor and rejecting the proud, the joy of those whom the world ignores and who have the Lord with them; everything that the song proclaims is the same as the teaching proclaimed in the beatitudes and the sermon on the mount. The very prelude expresses the tone and accent characteristic of the preaching of Jesus; the mother's song foreshadows the hymn of thanksgiving uttered by the Son in the presence of God who showers the lowly and humble with favors. *At that time Jesus answered and said: "I thank you, Father, Lord of heaven and earth, because you have hidden these things from the wise and prudent and have revealed them to little ones. Yes, Father, for so it has seemed good in your sight."* As we hear Christ in his mother, we also hear in her the entire Old Testament, which is a prefigure of Christ.

Theology of the Mystical Body, page 185ff

Ronald A. Knox (1881-1951), famous for his English translation of the Bible, wrote on a wide range of subjects. His thought is often strikingly original and his style characterized by his wit. In a sermon he speaks about Mary's immaculate conception as a sign of spring.

Our Lady is the culmination of that long process of selection, of choosing here and rejecting there a human instrument suited to his purpose, which is so characteristic of God's dealings with his ancient people. I think we can observe, throughout the whole of that process, two principles at work. One is that God chooses, every now and again, the unlikely candidate, the one we should not have chosen; chooses the younger son rather than the elder, the despised character rather than the prominent character. You see, he will shew us that grace is free; that his choice falls upon this human instrument or that without any antecedent merits on their part to account for it. And at the same time, he proves that his choice was justified; as the history of their dealings unfolds itself, we realize that the unlikely candidate was the right candidate, corresponds with the grace given and, not under compulsion but with free election of the will, seconds God's purposes and proves a ready accomplice for his salutary design. God's grace and man's free will corresponding with it — that ancient mystery is illustrated at every turn of the Old Testament story, until at last we turn over the page into the New Testament and find its ideal illustration in the life of our Lady herself.

By two separate streams the blood of David came down to Zorobabel, the hero of Israel's return from captivity. After that, it will have crossed and recrossed; we cannot even tell for certain the name of Saint Joseph's father. Nor do we know in what degree of relationship Saint Joseph stood to our blessed Lady. We only know that somehow, through cadet branches, that royal lineage came down to the second Eve, and the cycle of Old Testament history was complete. To what had the divine promises looked forward? To David, the man after God's own heart? To Solomon, the wisest of all princes? To Zorobabel, the deliverer of his people? No, to one village girl, a shepherd's daughter and a carpenter's bride. She is the culmination of all that process; for in her human nature reached to its highest dignity, to greet the divine condescension of the Incarnate. In her, as nowhere else, God had found the human instrument suited to his purpose; the worthy receptacle of a grace that had not dwelt on earth since Adam lost his paradise. The work of selection is consummated; mankind stands ready for its Redeemer.

A Retreat for Priests 17, pages 169-172

Frances Caryll Houselander (1901-1954) who worked in the censorship office in England during World War II wrote powerful and original works of spirituality on the theme of the suffering Christ in people. Her books became bestsellers; from 1942 onward doctors sent her their patients, children and adults, for therapy. In this passage she speaks intimately and profoundly about a mother's loss of a child. This applies especially to the Mother of Jesus.

Every woman who sees her child, every woman who is separated from her child, every woman who must stand by helpless and see her child die, every woman who echoes the old cry, "Why, why, why my child?" has the answer from the Mother of Christ. She can look at the child through Mary's eyes, she can know the answer with Mary's mind, she can accept the suffering with Mary's will, she can love Christ in her child with Mary's heart — because Mary has made her a mother of Christ. It is Christ who suffers in her child; it is his innocence redeeming the world, his love saving the world. He too is about his Father's business, the business of love.

Suffering is the price of love. The hardest thing but the inevitable thing in the suffering of every individual is that he must inflict his own suffering on those who love him.

It is love that redeems, love that can heal the world, love that can save it. Suffering has no power in itself; it is only powerful to save when it is caused by love, and when it is the expression of love.

The Mother of Christ loved the world with his love. She loved those who would be born into the world generations hence, those among whom are you and I. Witness the lyrical song of her love for us, ringing down the centuries from the first advent: *Behold, from this day forward all generations will count me blessed.*

Mary rejoiced because her child was to bring joy into the world, was to flood the world with his love.

The cause of Christ's suffering was his love for the world; the suffering he gave to his Mother was the gift of his own love. The increase of Christ's own grief because he must afflict her was an increase of Christ-love in the whole world — the suffering which is a communion of love.

Compassion, the communion in suffering of those who love, is the suffering that redeems; it is Christ's love in the world; it exists only because people love one another, and because it exists it begets more love.

Christ goes on his way; no word is spoken now; Mary follows him in the crowd. Another woman has anointed his feet for his burial; another will meet him on the way and wipe the blood and dirt from his face; others will weep aloud for him. Mary remains silent, she does not lift a hand; only when he is suffering no more will she anoint his body. She simply accepts this supreme gift of his love, his suffering given to her.

The Way of the Cross, pages 46-48

Pope Pius XII (1876-1958) defined the dogma of the Assumption on 1 November 1950. What was believed, written about, and speculated for centuries was declared an article of faith.

The venerable Mother of God, united with Jesus Christ in a mysterious way from all eternity "in one and the same decree" of predestination, in her conception immaculate, a virgin inviolate in her divine motherhood, a noble associate of the divine Redeemer, who won complete victory over sin and its consequences, received at last the supreme culmination of her privileges: to be preserved from the corruption of the sepulcher, and, like her Son before her, with death vanquished, to be carried aloft in body and soul to the exalted glory of heaven, and there as queen to be resplendent at the right hand of her very own Son, the immortal King of the ages.

Therefore, after directing unceasing prayers of petition to God, and after invoking the light of the Spirit of truth, to the glory of the omnipotent God who lavished his special benevolence on Mary the virgin, to the honor of her Son, the immortal King of ages and victor over sin and death, to the increase in glory of this same venerable Mother, and to the joy and exultation of the whole Church, we, by the authority of our Lord Jesus Christ, of the blessed apostles Peter and Paul, and our own, pronounce, declare, and define it to be a dogma divinely revealed, that the Immaculate Mother of God, the ever Virgin Mary, when the course of her earthly life was run, was assumed in body and in soul to heavenly glory.

Apostolic Constitution, Munificentissimus Deus

Father James, O.F.M. Cap. (1897-1962) *spent his life in teaching dogma. In this passage he reflects on Mary as the ideal woman.*

In Mary we find the essence of womanhood so concentrated that the light of the ideal flows down from her to invest every woman with something of its splendor. That is no mere figure of speech, and it is, besides, a fact to which history itself bears witness. In Mary's perfection, by a certain communication of privilege, the woman of Christendom shared; she found a place she never occupied before Christ came to give her true emancipation. The explanation is not far to seek. It is the ideal which gives meaning to the actual. But Mary is the ideal of womanhood. When one speaks of the ideal it is, not infrequently, to emphasize the distance that lies between the actual and the ideal. But in Mary that distance has been traversed: she is the actualized ideal. So marvelous is the conjunction in her of virginity and motherhood that she has exhausted in herself, as it were, the very meaning of womanhood, enjoying the integrity which is what is meant by virginity, yet giving life by a maternity which makes her the human source of eternal life for humanity. So entirely the work of God's creative Spirit is Mary, so wedded to God's purposes in entire docility, so untouched by earth or anything that savors not of God, that her virginity flowers in a motherhood to which the life of all the living is related. The Virgin Mother not only represents the perfection of human personality but the very maternal power itself which lies at the source of the re-created universe.

The Mother of Jesus, pages 87-88

Gerald Vann (1906-1963) *of the Dominican Order, a teacher and administrator for many years, had the gift of conveying profound truths in a very readable way to the public. He writes about Mary's assumption some years after its definition.*

The doctrine of the Assumption is of supreme importance not only to Catholics but to all men and women because it means that there is still in the world, there will always be in the world, a voice to affirm and a power to defend the dignity and the ultimate glory of matter, of material things, of human flesh and blood, of the lovely mystery of human love, of the beauty which is the work of people's hands. There is a voice which affirms, there is a power which defends, all the material things which make life worthwhile; and they bid us be of good heart because we can hope in the end to achieve our own lives, full, rich, deep, unified, free, not by escaping from the flesh and material things, but by the healing and sanctifying of the flesh and material things.

In the greatest of the Church's definitions of doctrine concerning our Lady, the doctrine that she is the mother of God, it was her Son that the Church was defending. But she is also the mother of all men and women; and here, in this doctrine of her Assumption, it is *all* her sons and daughters that the Church is defending. Just as the figure of motherhood is at the very center of the earthly history of every human soul, of the earthly history of the human race, so the figure of this Maiden-Mother is at the very center of the eternal history of individuals and of the race.   *The Water and the Fire, pages 175-176*

Karl Adam (1876-1966), *a prolific writer who aimed to expose doctrine in a clear, succinct fashion, spent his whole life as a priest in research, teaching, and writing. He was professor of dogmatic theology at the University of Tübingen. In this passage he describes Mary as a person who gave totally of herself to God and sums up the reason for this book: "For centuries now the Church has pondered this angelic salutation, prayerfully and lovingly."*

We know little or nothing of Mary's early life, but from the moment that she appears upon the stage of history, Mary is irradiated with light: *Hail, full of grace, the Lord is with you, blessed are you among women.* No angel has ever spoken a greater or holier word than that of man or woman. For centuries now the Church has pondered this angelic salutation, prayerfully and lovingly, and has discovered continually in it new glories of Mary. And yet her mystery is still unexhausted. In the light of the same gospel story we see her as one who in the deep consciousness of her lowliness is full of ecstatic joy and rejoices in God her Savior and in him alone, and in the ardor of her maiden surrender and overmastering inspiration foresees and proclaims the amazing truth: *Behold, from henceforth all generations shall call me blessed.* None other grasped as she did, at once and at the very beginnings of the gospel, its revolutionary and triumphant power, and therefore the Church calls her "Queen of prophets." We know further that her whole subsequent life was lowliness and simplicity on the one hand, and on the other strong and joyful faith.

The Spirit of Catholicism, pages 113-114.116-117

Gertrude von le Fort (1876-1971) *contrasts Mary's role with the role of every mother for her child.*

The earthly mother received her child from God and, through God's grace, carried him in her womb and brought him into the world; like Mary, she presented him in the temple and offered him to God and, again like Mary, she found him in the temple.

Sooner or later, for every mother, the time will come when, like Mary, she will be *looking anxiously* for her child; and the time, even harder to bear, when she will hear him reply: *What have you to do with me?* No solitude is to be compared with the solitude of a mother, for the beloved being who leaves her is inseparable from her; *the sword that will pierce her own soul* cuts off her own flesh and empties her own blood. Thus, sooner or later, secretly or in full view, in every mother the face of the Mother of Sorrows, the image of the Pieta, shines through. The book of destiny has many ways of showing this suffering that is endured by mothers: in the child who, in accordance with the law of nature, goes off on his own; in the tragic estrangement of the generations; and, more tragic still, in the child who is lost for ever, whether by accident, disaster, or death. But, in terms of religion, all the sorrows endured by mothers have but one name: the cross.

La femme eternelle, pages 131-133

Ansfried Hulsbosch (1912-1973), *an Augustinian who studied and taught sacred scripture in Rome and in Holland, wrote on evolution and biblical thought. In this passage he reflects on Mary's yes in God's creative work.*

The creative work of God achieves a breakthrough at a decisive point only by means of the consenting receptivity of Mary. Each of us must allow the creative work of God to be completed in the whole of his life, through faith and through love in which faith works. The old person in us must make way for the new person which we shall be, but only by our own consent. In Mary the old *world* is called to arise to its completion in a new *world*. She is the voice of the universe looking forward to completion. Bernard of Clairvaux expresses this splendidly in his second sermon for Pentecost: "With justice are the eyes of all creation bent upon you, for in you and through you and out of you the loving hand of the Most High has newly created everything that he created."

Does all this square with the modest place occupied by Mary in the gospels? Why not? The great acts of God are consummated inconspicuously. We should do wrong to attribute to Mary a kind of omniscience or a striking activity. Her greatness lies singly and solely in her pure receptivity. She is not in competition with the sovereignty of God, but is the person who acknowledged this sovereignty in the most radical fashion. She is the greatest of the faithful, always wondering about her Son, and following him to the foot of the cross.   *God's Creation, page 165*

Archbishop Fulton J. Sheen (1895-1979) *was a famous preacher of the Catholic faith and an author of many books. In this passage he extols Mary as a servant of God.*

There is an intrinsic relation between the humility of Mary and the incarnation of the Son of God within. She whom the heavens could not contain now tabernacles the king of the heavens. The Most High looks on the lowliness of his handmaid.

Mary's self-emptying alone would not have been enough, had not he who is her God, her Lord and Savior *humbled himself.* Though the cup be empty, it cannot hold the ocean. People are like sponges. As each sponge can hold only so much water and then reaches a point of saturation, so every person can hold only so much of honor. After the saturation point is reached, instead of man's wearing the purple, the purple wears the man. It is always *after* the honor is accepted that the recipient moans in false humility: *Lord, I am not worthy.*

But here, after the honor is received, Mary, instead of standing on her privilege, becomes a servant-nurse of her aged cousin and, in the midst of that service, sings a song in which she calls herself the Lord's handmaid — or better still the bondswoman of God, a slave who is simply his property and one who has no personal will except his own. Selflessness is shown as the true self. *There was no room in the inn,* because the inn was filled. There was room in the stable, because there were no egos there — only an ox and an ass.

The World's First Love, page 37

Pope Paul VI (1897-1977) had a great devotion to Mary and mentioned her often in his discourses. In an apostolic letter on the Blessed Virgin he reminds the Church that devotion to Mary must be based on scripture. In this passage he extols Mary's holiness.

Christ is the only way to the Father, and the ultimate example to whom the disciple must conform his own conduct, to the extent of sharing Christ's sentiments, living his life and possessing his Spirit. The Church has always taught this and nothing in pastoral activity should obscure this doctrine. But the Church, taught by the Holy Spirit and benefiting from centuries of experience, recognizes that devotion to the Blessed Virgin, subordinated to worship of the divine Savior and in connection with it, also has a great pastoral effectiveness and constitutes a force for renewing Christian living. It is easy to see the reason for this effectiveness. Mary's many-sided mission to the People of God is a supernatural reality which operates and bears fruit within the body of the Church. One finds cause for joy in considering the different aspects of this mission and seeing how each of these aspects with its individual effectiveness is directed toward the same end, namely, producing in the children the spiritual characteristics of the firstborn Son. The Virgin's maternal intercession, her exemplary holiness, and the divine grace which is in her become for the human race a reason for divine hope.

Marialis cultus, 57

Karl Rahner (1904-1984), *a Jesuit and leading Catholic theologian, was professor of dogmatic theology in Innsbruck, Austria, and later in Munich, West Germany. His works are written with lucid elegance. In this passage Mary's yes brought into the realm of grace her motherhood, which has a role in the history of redemption and thus affects all believers.*

The Word was made flesh because a maiden of our race knelt down at the angel's message and in the freedom of her heart and with the total unconditional gift of herself said: Be it done to me according to thy word. God willed this freely given love of his creature as the means by which the eternal Word of the Father should enter the world to take this world up into his own life. That was the way he willed to come into this world. As a consequence, Mary, of the same race as ourselves, is the portal of eternal mercy, the gate of heaven, through which we are in fact saved and redeemed and taken up into the life of God.

The divine motherhood of the blessed Virgin is therefore God's grace alone, and her own act, inseparably. It is not simply a physical motherhood, it is her grace and her deed, placing her whole self, body and soul, at the service of God and his redemptive mercy to humankind. And since this divine motherhood — as an act of faith personally made — belongs intrinsically to the history of redemption, it gives Mary a real relationship to us, for we are living in the history of redemption which she has decisively influenced. She has a place in our creed and our piety.

Mary, Mother of the Lord, pages 59.61

Francis X. Durwell, Redemptorist, *wrote on the theme of Christ's resurrection. In this passage he emphasizes Mary's role in salvation history and the Church.*

The whole history of God's people has been lived by Mary. The beginning of her life belongs to the first moment of sacred history, and its end coincides with the final hour of that history, and every stage between these two poles has been covered by Mary. For sacred history began not with man's first sin, but in the moment of redemptive mercy and the first promise of salvation — and it was in that moment that Mary was born, when God put an enmity between the woman and the serpent. Sacred history will be complete when man is saved by grace even in his body, and at the end of her life Mary attained this final salvation. All the events which mark out the way from these two opposite ends are found summed up in the life of Mary: like the people as a whole, she bore in her flesh the seed of salvation, she gave birth to Christ, and was associated in the work of redemption, for her own salvation and the salvation of the world. Yet she only sums up the history of the Church under one aspect. All life tells us of sin and of grace. Mary is the image of humanity only in the history of its salvation, a sacred icon, as it were, of the Church.

She is not just a figure of the Church, its perfect representative; she is its personification. That is why Mary still sings: *My soul magnifies the Lord, and my spirit rejoices in God my savior. For he that is mighty has done great things to me.* In the Redeeming Christ, *pages 288-289*

Cardinal Josef Suenens *of Belgium writes powerful works, consecrated to promoting the apostolate and to co-responsibility in the Church. He also passes on to his readers or hearers very personal marian meditations.*

We do not have the right to prescribe the limits of divine action or to bypass intermediaries which he has freely chosen. It is God's right to love us with abundance and superabundance and to communicate to his creatures the glory to be his instruments. In God there is a place for all excess and it is only at our level that one economizes. Our filial devotion toward Mary is nothing but gratitude for the excess of divine love of which she is the living and permanent proof. It would be a grave error to consider marian piety as a useless surplus, obstructing our religion toward God.

Mary is, after Christ, the most signal of God's graces. *If only you recognized God's gift,* said Jesus to the Samaritan woman. In this gift is enclosed the gift of Mary, for the mystery of the Son encompasses that of his Mother. One must not hesitate to accept from the hands of God what we are thus offered. To each one of us God repeats in some way the angel's words to Joseph: *Have no fear about taking Mary as your wife. It is by the Holy Spirit that she has conceived this child.* It is necessary to receive this gift from above with humility: to welcome, with open heart, all the love of God invested in Mary, for her joy and ours.

Pastoralia, 2 December 1968

Pierre Grelot, a professor of sacred scripture, is well versed in the Bible. In this passage he clearly points out Mary's role in the Church.

There exists between Mary and the Church a special relation which has no equivalent elsewhere. In any attempt to define the meaning of the realities scattered throughout sacred history, Mary cannot be treated like any other personage, neither in the New Testament, nor a fortiori in the Old; her significance is unique. Not only was she the first member of the Church in point of time, but the position she occupies and the role she plays make her the perfect model of the mystery of the Church, in the realm of faith as in that of grace, both as virgin and as mother. It would be insufficient to call her the figure of the Church, if the word figure is given the same meaning it has for the personages and realities of the Old Testament. She is something greater and better than a figure. Next to Christ, in her humble position, she in some way personifies the Church, and it is not unintentional that the fourth gospel depicts her at the foot of the cross becoming by the will of Christ the mother of the beloved disciple who represents all Christians. Because she is the mother of Christ, because her maternal suffering associated her with the passion of her son, by virtue of the will of Christ she concretely personifies and signifies the maternity of the Church as its source, which is precisely the fruit of the cross. In a word, in Mary the mystery of the Church is positively revealed in its most perfect form.

La Bible, Parole de Dieu, pages 289-290

Réné Voillaume, a follower of Charles de Foucauld, writes about the union of Mary and Jesus, the greatest proof of Mary's love.

Mary reached the fulfillment of her faith at the time of the passion, and then another mystery takes place: the Virgin's mission, as the Mother of Jesus on earth, ends there because her Son has died. What more can she give her Son? She has nothing more to give him. But something yet deeper takes place in her, because when a mother sees her son die she cannot but experience the fullness of suffering, especially when she sees him die, not from a natural death, but young and condemned. We know well that if the greatest proof of love is to lay down our life for those we love, then the greatest suffering is also the greatest proof of love. And God puts her there so that she can give this greatest proof of love.

Her union with her Son is too great for there not to be a mystery of collaboration in this, because love does collaborate. The kind of "travail" which her Son effected for the redemption of the world enabled her, for the first time, to collaborate wholly. She experienced to the depth of her being that suffering which is redemptive suffering. And since there is no doubt but that at that moment she understood her Son's mission perfectly, you will realize what a unique place she has in the redemption of souls. She came there through an ordeal which is the paroxysm of a mother's suffering, and in full illumination of faith.

Demeures de Dieu: l'Eglise, la Vierge, pages 53-55

Réné Laurentin is the world's leading authority on mariology and has written much on the Mother of the Lord. In this passage the author reflects on Mary and the return of the Lord.

From the outset Mary had preceded the Church at every stage of its life, and here we see the Church joining her once more. Between them there is no longer any difference in the realm of place and time. The tension of nature over against heaven, of time over against eternity, has been abolished. At the end of the journey, there they are perfectly reunited in the place and at the time of which God is the measure.

Mary was the first personal realization of what awaits the redeemed. She is that still, but the distances have been done away with.

The Church continues to look at Mary in Christ, but in a different way: no longer as its future and as a token of its hope, but only as the summit of its communion in Christ. The Church used to look at Mary as a fleet in the storm looks at the first ship which has crossed the bar and reached port. Now, the Church has rejoined her at the end of the voyage. There is no longer either separation or distance, but common joy in reunion in Christ, and this dialogue between them is nothing but the overflowing abundance of their thanksgiving. In this communion, of which Christ is the beginning and the completion, we see again the situation of Pentecost: Mary in the Church, but beyond this world.

Court Traité sur la Vierge Marie, pages 156-157

Raymond Brown, *a Sulpician, is a distinguished biblical scholar who has done significant research on the Bible. In this passage he explains the woman and the disciple at the foot of the cross.*

At the foot of the cross there are brought together the two great symbolic figures of the fourth gospel whose personal names are never used by the evangelist: the mother of Jesus and the disciple whom Jesus loved. Both were historical personages, but they are not named by John, since their primary (not sole) importance is in their symbolism for discipleship rather than in their historical careers. During the ministry, as we saw in the final Johannine form of the Cana story, the mother of Jesus was denied involvement as his physical mother in favor of the timetable of the "hour" dictated by Jesus' Father; but now that the hour has come for Jesus to pass from this world to the Father, Jesus will grant her a role that will involve her, not as *his* mother but as the mother of the beloved disciple. In other words, John agrees with Luke that Jesus' rejection of intervention by Mary did not mean that his natural family could not become his true family through discipleship. By stressing not only that his mother has become the mother of the beloved disciple, but also that this disciple has become her son, the Johannine Jesus is logically claiming the disciple as his true brother. In the fourth gospel, then, as well as in the synoptic scene, Jesus has reinterpreted who his mother and his brothers are and reinterpreted them in terms of discipleship.

The Community of the Beloved Disciple, pages 196-197

Cardinal Joseph Ratzinger, Prefect of the Congregation for the Doctrine of the Faith, upholds Mary's faith in God.

Mary is the great believer who humbly offered herself to God as an empty vessel for him to use in his mysterious plan. Without complaint she surrendered control of her life; she did not try to live according to human calculation but put herself completely at the disposal of God's mysterious, incomprehensible design. All she wanted to be was the handmaid of the Lord, the instrument and servant of the Word. Therein lies her true fame: that she remained a believer despite all the darkness and all the inexplicable demands God made on her. She believed even in the face of certain incomprehensible facts: that she should carry her Creator in her womb; that the child growing there should be the Lord; that he who was the source of Israel's salvation should be regarded by his fellows as deranged; that he should brush her aside, first as a twelve year-old and again at the beginning of his public life; that he who was to bring salvation and healing to Israel should be executed by that same Israel.

Today God is still mysterious; indeed he seems to have a special kind of obscurity in store for each person's life. But could he ever render any life as dark and incomprehensible as he did Mary's? "Blessed are you who have believed," even when this faith became a sword that pierced her heart. This is the real reason for her greatness and her being called blessed: she is the great believer.

The Visitation of Mary, pages 110-111

Edward Schillebeeckx, *a Dominican and theologian, wrote much on church, sacraments, and Mary. In this passage he shows how Mary's fiat had repercussions for her and for us.*

Our devotion to Mary must go right to the heart of the living Christian faith. It must be a *fiat* which goes, in sacrificial love, to the ultimate limit. Life is only good if it is offered as a gift. Life is love, a love which gives. The gift which we make of our love, our life, must be made in a spirit of pure self-forgetfulness. If we do this, our suffering will become a relic of Christ's redeeming death, a priceless relic which will find its resting-place, like the crucified Christ's, in the arms of Mary, his and our mother. She will take the racked treasure of our suffering on her knees and place it beside the tortured relic of Christ's body. Her lap contains all the suffering of the whole of humanity, the countless, ever-growing number of wounds of a human race which is continuously crucified. She is the great *Pieta* who casts her mother's cloak of mercy over our suffering humanity. She is the living womb in which, as in a second act of bodily motherhood, we are carried for the nine long months of our lives until we at last come to the glory of redemption and resurrection.

Mary is the loving heart in our lives. She is objective and even matter-of-fact, but, because she has herself experienced and shared them, she always understands our difficulties in life and has sympathy for us. With unfailing solicitude she finds out what our needs are and, with the straightforward simplicity of a mother, she brings them to the attention of God who, in Jesus, was and still is her Child, her "Boy" — "They have no wine!"

Mary, Mother of the Redemption, pages 174-175

Pope John Paul II, who proclaimed 1987-1988 a marian year, has always cultivated a devotion to Mary. On his first apostolic pilgrimage to the United States in 1979 he spoke of Mary at the National Shrine of the Immaculate Conception in Washington, DC.

In the eternal design of God, this woman, Mary, was chosen to enter into the work of the incarnation and redemption. This design of God was to be actuated through her free decision given in obedience to the divine will. Through her "yes," a "yes" that pervades and is reflected in all history, she consented to be the Virgin Mother of our saving God, the handmaid of the Lord, and at the same time, the Mother of all the faithful who in the course of the centuries would become brothers and sisters of her Son. Through her, the Sun of Justice was to rise in the world. Through her, the great healer of humanity, the reconciler of hearts and consciences, her Son, the God-Man, Jesus Christ, was to transform the human condition and by his death and resurrection uplift the entire human family. As a great sign that appeared in the heavens, in the fullness of time, this woman dominates all history as the Virgin Mother of the Son and as the Spouse of the Holy Spirit, as the Handmaid of humanity.

This woman becomes also, by association with her Son, the sign of contradiction to the world, and at the same time the sign of hope, whom all generations shall call blessed.

The woman who conceived spiritually before she conceived physically, the woman who accepted the Word of God, the woman who was inserted intimately and irrevocably into the mystery of the Church, exercises a spiritual motherhood with regard to all peoples. The woman who is honored as Queen of Apostles, without herself being inserted into the hierarchical constitution of the Church — this woman made all hierarchy possible because she gave to the world the Shepherd and Bishop of our souls. This woman, this Mary of the gospels, who is not mentioned as being at the Last Supper, comes back again at the foot of the cross, in order to consummate her contribution to salvation history. By her courageous act she prefigures and anticipates the courage of all women throughout the ages who concur in bringing forth Christ in every generation.

At Pentecost, the Virgin Mother once again comes forward to exercise her role in union with the apostles, with and in and over the Church. Yet again, she conceived of the Holy Spirit to bring forth Jesus in the fullness of his body, the Church, never to leave him, never to abandon him, but to continue to love and to cherish him through the ages.

This is the woman of history and destiny who inspires us today, the woman who speaks to us of femininity, human dignity, and love, and who is the greatest expression of total consecration to Jesus Christ.

Discourses, 7 October 1979

Epilogue

From the texts and descriptions we see that as the Church traveled through history so did devotion to Mary, the Mother of God. And this devotion always led to some event: a council, a dogma, an apparition, etc.

As we prepare our entry into the twenty-first century what will devotion to Mary bring? No one knows. However, we do know that her most venerated and revered title will last from century to century:

Mary, the Mother of God
Theotokos

At the end of the nineteenth century Pope Leo XIII, who had a great devotion to Mary under the title of Our Mother of Good Counsel, summed up well marian thought at that particular time: "Mary accepted with a magnanimous heart this great and laborious function of mother and from the time in the cenacle we see her supporting admirably the firstfruits of the Christian people with the sanctity of her examples, the authority of her counsels, the gentleness of her consolations, the efficacy of her prayers" (Encyclical, 5 September 1895).

Mary's yes will continue to resound from age to age.

Index of Authors